Write Fantastic Non-f
And Get It Published

I dedicate this book to my husband, Nick and my two sons, Alex and George. And to every new writer who has the courage to commit their thoughts to paper and to share them with a wider world.

Teach Yourself®

Write Fantastic Non-fiction And Get It Published

Claire Gillman

For order enquiries: please contact Bookpoint Ltd,
130 Milton Park, Abingdon, Oxon OX14 4SB.
Telephone: +44 (0) 1235 827720. Fax: +44 (0) 1235 400454.
Lines are open 09.00–17.00, Monday to Saturday, with a 24-hour
message answering service. Details about our titles and how to
order are available at www.teachyourself.com

Long renowned as the authoritative source for self-guided
learning – with more than 50 million copies sold worldwide – the
Teach Yourself series includes over 500 titles in the fields of
languages, crafts, hobbies, business, computing and education.

British Library Cataloguing in Publication Data: a catalogue
record for this title is available from the British Library.

First published in UK 2011 by Hodder Education, part
of Hachette UK, 338 Euston Road, London NW1 3BH.

The **Teach Yourself** name is a registered trade mark of
Hodder Headline.

Typeset by MPS Limited, a Macmillan Company.

Printed in Great Britain for Hodder Education, an Hachette UK
Company, 338 Euston Road, London NW1 3BH, by CPI Cox &
Wyman, Reading, Berkshire RG1 8EX.

The publisher has used its best endeavours to ensure that the URLs
for external websites referred to in this book are correct and active
at the time of going to press. However, the publisher and the author
have no responsibility for the websites and can make no guarantee
that a site will remain live or that the content will remain relevant,
decent or appropriate.

Hachette UK's policy is to use papers that are natural, renewable
and recyclable products and made from wood grown in sustainable
forests. The logging and manufacturing processes are expected to
conform to the environmental regulations of the country of origin.

Impression number   10 9 8 7 6 5 4 3 2 1
Year   2015 2014 2013 2012 2011

Acknowledgements

Warm thanks and appreciation to Chelsey Fox and Victoria Roddam, and to all the writers and students who have inspired me, taught me and helped contribute to this project.

Contents

Meet the author

I have been writing professionally for over 25 years and I love what I do. Writing can be fun and fulfilling, yet frustrating and challenging in equal measure, but it is always interesting. I have interviewed some amazing people and I have written about subjects that I have found fascinating and that I hope inspire a similar response in my readers.

As a staff journalist, I have edited consumer magazines specializing in health, parenting and travel – all of which are subjects close to my heart. As a freelancer, I contribute to women's magazines and national newspapers. I have written over a dozen non-fiction books for adults and a series of creative non-fiction titles for children under the pen name, Rory Storm. The longer deadlines of the books dovetail nicely with the immediacy of writing for magazines and newspapers.

I am also an editor for Writers' Workshop, specializing in non-fiction. It is hugely rewarding to be able to help new writers to get their ideas and writing into shape for possible publication. For that reason, I also love to run writing courses and groups; it is inspiring, fun and fulfilling at the same time. If you would care to join me, details can be found at www.clairegillman.com

Writing non-fiction for a living has allowed me to lead the life I always wanted. I live on the edge of the West Pennine moors with my family and dog and combine the huge pleasure of writing with an outdoor lifestyle.

In one minute

Non-fiction is a genre of writing that is often over-shadowed by its sexier cousin, fiction. Yet non-fiction is an amazingly comprehensive and versatile style of writing, and creatively it can be just as fulfilling as fiction.

You only have to look at the breadth of sub-genres within non-fiction to see that there is bound to be a suitable outlet for your writing talents. Whether you want to inform and pass on knowledge through self-help and 'how to' books, or to record family stories for future generations by writing a memoir or family history, or to entertain and inform through creative non-fiction, travel writing and specialist areas such as history, there is plenty of scope for the non-fiction writer.

You are also spoilt for choice in terms of which vehicle you choose to present your non-fiction work. You can go down the traditional route of having your writing published in a magazine or book, or broadcast on radio or television, and publishing opportunities for works of non-fiction are more plentiful than for fiction. Alternatively, new media has opened up further opportunities to share your writing through blogging, e-books and self-publishing.

Some non-fiction writers prefer to keep their writing private – and that is fine too. Because ultimately, it is the process of writing – the research, the editing, the perfecting of your words, and producing a final manuscript – that is the greatest joy and the most liberating and fulfilling aspect of non-fiction writing.

1

Why write non-fiction?

In this chapter you will learn:
- *how this book can help you*
- *about the breadth of opportunities*
- *what's in it for you, the writer.*

It is said that everyone has a book in them but it is not always a novel. From my experience as a non-fiction editor, I know that there is no shortage of people who are keen to share their knowledge or who want to tell their true story in print to a wide audience.

The umbrella term of non-fiction writing covers such a broad spectrum of different genres, ranging from self-help and 'how to' books through travel and memoir writing, to journalism and writing for television and radio. There are so many exciting opportunities and different media through which you can communicate your message or express your story, some of which you may be familiar with; others may be new to you but, when you find out more about them, they might be the perfect platform for you to convey your message.

Although magazine and book publishing have been hard hit by the economic climate, in many ways, there could not be a better time to be a non-fiction writer. That's because, in addition to the traditional routes to publication, there are now many more options on offer to help you to make your non-fiction writing available to the public: self-publishing, print-on-demand publishing (POD), e-books, podcasts and blogs are just some of the latest choices available to the budding author. Even if getting published is not your ultimate aim, personal writing and creative non-fiction can offer incredible insights and profound discoveries to the non-fiction writer.

Yet despite encouraging developments in the publishing world – and even though you may believe you 'have a book in you' and a strong desire to see it published – you may be finding it hard to progress beyond the concept stage. If this is the case, then *Write Fantastic Non-fiction And Get It Published* can help.

What's stopping you?

Have you always wanted to write? Do you have something important to say or have specialist knowledge in a certain field? Have you spotted a gap in the publishing market that you want to fill?

All of these scenarios, and more, are good reasons to want to write non-fiction. So what is holding you back from starting to write? Most new writers say that they find it hard to find the time to write. Others are afraid that their writing will not be good enough. Some simply do not know where to start. Whatever your particular reason for putting off your writing project, you now have all the tools at your disposal to get started and to see your writing project through from its inception to publication.

How can this book help you?

Sometimes the prospect of taking on a big writing project can seem so overwhelming that you put off writing your book indefinitely. However, *Write Fantastic Non-fiction And Get It Published* can:

- ▶ help you to turn your ideas into books
- ▶ help you to select your subject
- ▶ help you to hone your research and writing skills
- ▶ help you to explore a range of genres and styles
- ▶ help you to identify publishing choices
- ▶ help you to find an editor, publisher or agent
- ▶ help to give you confidence.

Undoubtedly there is luck involved in getting published. Success can sometimes rely on something as tenuous as your proposal falling on the desk of the right agent or editor at the right time and being just what they are looking for. However, luck aside, there are numerous things that you can do to make sure you get your book and proposal right, and that it goes to the right person, and this book can help you to achieve that.

How to use this book

Write Fantastic Non-fiction And Get It Published will guide you through the various steps to completing your writing project and, if you so desire, there is also insider advice on the best way to find a publisher or agent. Although the book covers many different genres of writing, the same advice applies whether you are writing non-fiction to make a name for yourself, to help others, to make money or to fulfil a personal ambition.

The early chapters Selecting your subject, Researching your project, Starting to write and Revision and rewriting apply to all genres of non-fiction writing. It is entirely up to you, but it is probably advisable to read these in succession.

Subsequent chapters are dedicated to specific types of non-fiction writing. You can cherry-pick the chapters that apply specifically to your writing project or you may find that if you read them all, something previously unconsidered will resonate with you, and your project takes on a new form or different direction.

The final chapters are aimed at helping you to decide which route to publication is the right one for you. Perhaps the new media opportunities are worth considering, even if you have not previously given them thought. Alternatively, if you go down the traditional publishing path, there is advice on whether you should submit directly to a publisher or find an agent.

At the end of every chapter, there are suggested exercises that will help to develop your writing skills and build confidence. You do not have to attempt all or any of these exercises, but if you do, you may find that they give you ideas and greater fluency in your writing. Even if the exercise is for a different genre from your own project, many of the skills are transferable; what is useful for the travel writer could also be beneficial to those experimenting with creative non-fiction, for example.

Whether or not you choose to participate in the exercises, I would strongly recommend that in general you write as much as you can.

It does not have to be specifically for your chosen project, but time invested in practising the written word is never lost. If you can practise and hone your writing skills in as many ways as possible, it will help you on your journey to getting published.

What you will gain

I have drawn on my own experience from a writing career that spans journalism, broadcasting, publishing, editing and teaching to inform the practical advice in this book. As a writing consultant/coach, the valuable insights I have gained from working closely with new writers also gave me ideas as to what to include. However, even though there are some practical exercises and lots of useful advice, it is not a substitute for writing practice or a specialized writing course if you suspect that your writing is not up to scratch.

This is not an exhaustive guide to every single aspect of non-fiction writing, but what it can do is help you to tackle a non-fiction writing project in the most effective and time-economical way possible. My aim is to ensure that you have the tools to create non-fiction writing that is saleable, whether or not you decide to go down the route of writing non-fiction for a living or getting your writing published.

If you want to be a non-fiction writer it requires a certain amount of dedication and self-discipline, the ability to work on your own, an eye for detailed and in-depth research but, above all else, a love of the written word is absolutely essential. You must enjoy committing your ideas and findings to paper (metaphorically), tweaking and re-jigging your writing until the words sound just right, and playing creatively with the musicality of what you are saying. Good writing together with abundant enthusiasm for your subject will shine through your prose and inspire your readers.

Whether you see writing non-fiction as an absorbing and fulfilling hobby, as a way of passing on knowledge or an important message, or as a way to earn a living in the future, I hope that the information in this book will help you to achieve your goals and give you the tools you need.

2

Selecting your subject

In this chapter you will learn:
- *how to come up with ideas*
- *where to seek inspiration*
- *how to develop ideas.*

Generating ideas

Most people feel they have a book in them, so they say, but identifying what that book should be about is often the hardest part of getting published. Whether you want to write non-fiction for magazines or books, the point at which many authors falter is deciding on an initial idea to commit to paper.

The good news is that there are techniques for helping you to generate ideas and to identify which ones are worth pursuing. If you are struggling to come up with subject matter, don't be too concerned: it's not writers' block or lack of imagination. It's more a case of not knowing how to tap in to the rich source of material that is at your fingertips. By adopting some of the following suggestions, you will be on the right path to inspiration.

WAITING FOR INSPIRATION

If you are waiting for that wonderful light bulb moment when an original and outstanding idea comes to you, you are probably waiting in vain. As the author Jack London pointed out, 'You can't wait for inspiration. You have to go after it with a club.'

Perhaps there will come a day when the big idea hits you but, initially, don't try to come up with something ground breaking, just something that you can use to form the basis of an article or book. As you start to actively search out ideas, you will be surprised at just how much material is available to you. In the same way, once your antennae become more highly attuned to what could make a good feature or book idea, the whole process snowballs and the ideas start to flood in. This is why people who make a living out of coming up with ideas, such as writers and advertising executives, never seem to have a shortage of new project suggestions and new book titles.

Writing about what you know

It may sound hackneyed to say 'Write about what you know', but it is nonetheless true: your first port of call when looking for inspiration is always to look at your own life. Obviously, it is important that you have some expertise or experience in a certain subject before you can write about it, but that does not mean you have to be a leading expert in the field. It simply means you have to have relevant personal life experience in order firstly to convince a publisher/magazine editor and secondly, so that you sound authoritative and informative to a reader. If in doubt about it, just ask yourself, 'Do I know what I'm talking about?'

The pitfall with this question is that your inner self-critic is likely to play down what you have to offer. Don't be over-critical here. If you work in a specific field or have wide experience of a certain sport or hobby, there is a good chance that you have a rich supply of material and a wealth of knowledge that could be of great interest to a more general readership.

Insight – is there a market?

Without wishing to sound unduly pessimistic, there is a caveat to the requirement that you are interested in what you write about. And that is that other people find the subject interesting too. Fundamentally, there have to be enough people sufficiently interested in the topic to pay say £9.99 for a copy of your book in order to learn more about the subject.

FRIENDS, FAMILY AND COLLEAGUES

You will undoubtedly know people who have undergone exceptional experiences in their lives, whether it is surviving a disaster or serious illness, or an amazing feat of endurance. Perhaps an interview with them could form the basis of a feature that you submit to a relevant publication. If there is enough depth to their story, could it be the subject of a book? Perhaps it is one of your family forebears who has led a remarkable life and who interests you. The number of people researching their family history has boomed with the advent of research tools such as the internet. When the 1901 census for England and Wales went online in 2002, it received 50 million hits on the first day and subsequently crashed. Colourful characters from the past can be a rich source of material for the non-fiction writer.

DO YOU FIND IT INTERESTING?

This may sound an odd question but you would be surprised how many people attempt to write about a subject upon which they are quite knowledgeable but which actually is of no interest to them. It is not then surprising that the copy is flat and lifeless. If you have spent 15 years in practice as a dentist and you are a keen potholer in your spare time, are you going to write a book on dentistry or potholing? Which subject lights your fire? You have to have a passion for your chosen topic because this translates on to the page.

Bear in mind that if you are lucky enough to publish a successful book, then there is every chance that you will be talking about its subject matter in interviews on local radio and in the press. If it is in a specialist field, you might even be asked to write articles or to give seminars and lectures. Moreover, once your book is published, your publisher may invite you to write a follow-up title or to create related companion volumes, since every publishing house knows that it is easier to sell an additional book to an existing reader than to find a new customer. This means that you could be writing and talking on this subject for several years to come, so it is important that it is a topic that interests you.

Insight – specialist knowledge can hit the right mark
In the early 1990s, as a keen skier with young children, I noticed that the specialist ski magazines were not catering for families. I submitted some feature ideas and ended up writing regularly for *Daily Mail Ski* magazine. Our experience of skiing with small children was considered useful specialist knowledge by the editor.

Finding a fresh angle

Once you have identified an idea on a subject in which you have expertise or experience, then it is important to come up with a fresh angle. Don't worry if there are already books in print on the subject – remember there is nothing new under the sun – but how you present the topic is important. The range of topics for non-fiction books is enormous, with demand for 'how to' and personal development in particular growing in recent years. One of the biggest publishing phenomena in recent years – with global sales of over 40 million copies in over 45 languages throughout the world – is John Gray's book *Men are from Mars, Women are from Venus*. It is not that books about the differences between the genres have not been written before, but the angle that men and women are so different they might as well come from different planets was completely original. It was a concept that people could grasp straight away.

NOT TOO GENERAL

This may sound counter-intuitive but tailoring a book's appeal to a specialized target audience will actually increase sales. How? By knowing your audience and by focusing the information closely to their (and your) interests, it means that more readers will identify with its content and buy it.

If you doubt the wisdom of this, you have only to look at the magazine market. In the 1980s, I briefly edited a general cycling magazine – imaginatively entitled *Bicycle Magazine* – which looked at all aspects of the cycling scene. It is no longer in circulation; instead enthusiasts can now choose from a plethora of specialist magazines devoted variously to road cycling, mountain biking, BMX biking and more.

Techniques to aid inspiration

Inspiration is notoriously capricious, but here are some tried and tested techniques that can help you to generate countless ideas for articles and books.

BRAINSTORMING

This is a very useful technique for generating ideas. You simply sit down with a blank sheet of paper in front of you and try to write down as many ideas as possible. Don't think about it too much – whatever comes into your head, just commit it to paper without mentally judging its merit first. (If you start evaluating ideas before you write them down, you will interrupt your flow of thought.)

Don't worry if the ideas jump about, just get them down in whichever order they occur to you.

The sifting process can come later but don't be too quick to judge. An idea that at first glance might strike you as outlandish may, with a little consideration and adaptation, become the kernel of a feature or book concept.

VISUAL BRAINSTORMING

There is a system of visualizing brainstorming sessions that has been used by management experts since the 1990s, and which is very helpful to writers. It is really an extension of the brainstorming process, if you like.

You put your central theme in a bubble in the centre of a blank piece of paper and then the main ideas associated with it are written around this key concept and linked to it by lines or arrows. Sub-headings then cluster around the relevant main idea and, if they link to another idea, you draw an arrow or line between them. Although it sounds haphazard, the elements of brainstorming process will be arranged intuitively, depending on the importance you give to certain concepts.

By drawing your ideas in a non-linear manner, it encourages a brainstorming approach to generating ideas that disrupts the prioritizing of concepts which often happens when you write lists, for example. As you can see in Figure 2.1, when I was working out the content of my book *A Green Guide to your Natural Pregnancy and Birth*, I wrote the title in the middle of my diagram and then radiated out potential subjects for the various chapters. Then from those chapter headings, I added topics that I thought should be included within each chapter. This system works well for me when I need to marshal my thoughts about a book project, but when I'm after general ideas or looking for inspiration, I tend to rely on brainstorming.

READ VORACIOUSLY

You can get a lot of good ideas from reading newspapers and magazines. Once you are familiar with the type of articles that a magazine covers or the sort of books that a publisher has on its list, you can start to think about something in a similar vein that you are well placed to produce. For example, if you know a certain magazine regularly carries a health story focusing on real-life experiences,

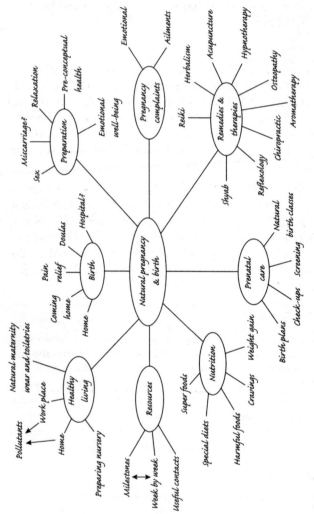

Figure 2.1 Example brainstorm diagram.

you might be able to interest them in an article about your dad's Alzheimer's disease and how your sister gave up work to care for him. Perhaps in the sample story that you read, the case study was on a child with diabetes, but this could be enough to stimulate the idea that your feature might fit into that particular slot and be of interest to the editor.

WRITE IT DOWN

The vast majority of writers that I know keep a notebook full of ideas. Personally, I like the whole ritual of writing, so I always treat myself to a beautifully bound, hardback A4 notebook in which I will write ideas for features and books. In reality, any style of notebook will do – you can even use file cards kept in a box – as long as you know where to lay your hands on your book/file box when you have an idea to jot down.

It's also handy to take a smaller notebook or voice recorder with you when you are out and about, as long as you don't forget to then transfer your idea in to your 'official' notebook when you get home. I've even been known to call my home phone or my mobile, and to leave an answerphone message, which I later transcribe, so that I do not let a good idea that strikes me while I'm travelling slip through my fingers.

Insight – dream inspiration

Like many writers, I always keep a notepad beside my bed so that I can jot down any ideas that come to me in the night as dreams. In that early morning half-awake, half-asleep state, you think you'll remember, but dreams are elusive and you may well forget the detail if you don't commit it to paper immediately.

INSPIRATION EXERCISE

There is no one else in this world who can draw on exactly the same range of experiences or cast of characters from your lifetime. So, why not surprise yourself by trying this exercise for finding inspiration from the things and people you know.

Take five large sheets of paper and at the top of each sheet write one of the following categories as a heading:

- Yourself
- People
- Places
- Hobbies/pastimes
- Career

Now brainstorm ideas around each topic, jotting them down at random as they come to you. Don't edit out anything at this stage. Simply write the ideas down and, if you need more space, continue on the back or on a new sheet of paper.

Just to get you started, here are a few angles you might like to think about:

Yourself

- Are you married or single? How do you like it?
- Do you have children? What's interesting about them?
- Do you have any health conditions?

People

- Do your friends or family do anything unusual or exceptional?
- Do they have any health issues?
- Are any of them well known/famous for anything?

Places

- Have you lived in any interesting locations?
- Where have you been on holiday that has most interested you?
- Have you undertaken any unusual journeys or used noteworthy modes of transport?

Hobbies/pastimes

- What do you do in your spare time?
- Can you share any specialist knowledge?

- ▶ Is there any aspect of your hobby that is unique to you (for example, participants are usually the opposite gender)?
- ▶ Are you on speaking terms with any leading lights in the field? Could you interview them?

Career

- ▶ Do you have any specialist career knowledge to share?
- ▶ List all of your previous work experience and what it involved.
- ▶ Can you recall any interesting colleagues?

These are simply ideas to get you started and I'm sure you can come up with many more questions. You may well be surprised by the abundance of material that is thrown up by this unfamiliar self-scrutiny.

3

Researching your project

In this chapter you will learn:
- *how to research your idea*
- *how to use different resources*
- *how to make sure your sources are reliable.*

Do I have a viable idea?

Once you have decided upon an idea, the next step is to do some preliminary research to find out whether there is enough material available to support a feature or a book. After a trawl of the internet and newspaper cuttings, you have to ask yourself if there is anything new to say on the subject or alternatively do you have a new angle of approach. If the answer is 'Yes' to either of these questions, you can start to research in earnest.

Finding material

You will need to gather as much information as possible from various sources to inform and flesh out your feature or book. You can never have too much research material – although it can be a lengthy process when you eventually go through the pile working out what is of most relevance and practical use. Finding good research material in the first place is also a time-consuming exercise and one of the most engrossing parts of the writing process. However, it is an essential task if your non-fiction writing is to have an authoritative and informed style.

Luckily for the non-fiction writer, with today's communication networks, there has never been an easier time to research your project.

You have countless resources to call upon, and in my experience, it is worth trying them all. Alternatively, you can cherry-pick the resource that best suits your chosen field of writing and use that almost exclusively. For example, if you are writing about one of your great-grandfathers, it might be enough to concentrate on genealogy websites, the local history section of your local library and/or second-hand bookshops and interviews with family members. Looking at national newspaper archives would probably be a waste of your time, unless your great-grandfather was famous, infamous or did something remarkable. Here are some of the resources that you can use in your quest for background material.

THE INTERNET

The world wide web is an almost inexhaustible supply of research material on every topic imaginable. It also offers the most up to date information available. However, you have to exercise some caution when using the information highway as a research tool. Firstly, you must make sure that your source is reliable. Anyone can post information on the internet and sometimes what you find is opinion or speculation rather than fact. If you find something that you think is useful but you are not sure about its accuracy, try to cross-reference it against another source. The most reliable sources of specialist information are the professional organizations, governing bodies and leading charities in the field. In addition, always check the date that the information is posted. There is no sense in believing that you are writing about cutting edge developments if the startling revelations on the site were posted in 2004.

Once you have found a website that is of interest, there is no reason why you should not contact the site creator with further questions if it does not have all the answers that you are looking for. As a case in point, a few years ago, I wrote a children's book on cryptozoology (the study of rumoured or mythological animals, such as the yeti, that are presumed to exist, but for which conclusive proof does not yet exist). While researching the book, I found myself corresponding with a cryptozoology enthusiast who had posted a very interesting and useful website. I asked several questions and the website creator then contacted other experts within this small but fascinating group of enthusiasts and experts. He was later able to furnish me with the information I needed and, on the questions that he could not answer himself, he was able to point me towards another resource that proved equally useful.

Undoubtedly, you can end up spending a lot of time looking for information on the internet. As you follow up one lead, it often takes you to several more. Although in general the people that you find through the internet can be generous with their time and their knowledge, there are others on the web who are less scrupulous. Given that you will be hitting countless unknown websites, it is therefore a sensible precaution to make sure you have a good firewall and virus checker installed on your computer before you start internet researching in earnest.

> **Insight – keep your sources to hand**
> When using the internet to research a writing project, I set up a folder in 'Favourites' or 'Bookmarks' and add all the websites that have useful information. In that way, if an editor or publisher asks for sources, you have them at your fingertips. It's also helpful to have them stored in one place when it comes to compiling a 'Further information' page or box.

BOOKS

Despite the popularity of the internet, books are a valuable resource for the non-fiction writer and should not be overlooked. If you are writing about your specialist hobby or pastime, there is a good chance you will already have books on the topic on your bookshelf that will be worth revisiting. You can also borrow specialist books from friends who share the same fascination for this subject. Although it can be a costly exercise to buy research books, if you plan to continue to write in a specific field, then these books are an investment, and you will soon build up a useful reference library that you can call upon time and again.

If this investment is not an option for you, then public lending libraries can be a good alternative. Not only are librarians good at finding relevant books on a given topic, they can also order a specific book for you, if it is in stock in one of the branches of their library network. On occasions, the library can even order a new book on your behalf. There are also specialist libraries, which you will probably know about if you are writing as an expert or enthusiast in a specialized field.

MAGAZINES AND NEWSLETTERS

Contact the back issue department of specialist magazines, as they can be very helpful in locating articles on your chosen subject.

For example, if you are writing for a niche market, such as Italian motorbikes, then contacting the editors of the newsletters/magazines for the Ducati, Laverda and Benelli owners clubs could prove a useful source of first-hand knowledge.

NEWSPAPER ARCHIVES

Local lending libraries often hold local newspaper archives stored on microfiche. The librarian should be happy to show you how to use this system if it is unfamiliar to you. National newspapers have online archives that you can search for free in some instances. Others charge for this service but it can be a useful source of information. In addition, newspaper articles often contain interviews with leading specialists, so can also be a good lead for names of relevant experts in the field.

Insight – travel writing sources

When writing any form of travel feature, embassies and national travel services are an amazing mine of information and a great source of contacts. In my experience, members of staff are normally extremely helpful too.

Interview techniques

Introducing the voice of an expert or the narrative of a real-life case story into an article can lift your writing and add interest or gravitas in equal measure. So do not be afraid to interview people in the course of your research, as it can be a powerful addition to the facts and statistics that you unearth. For preference, you should interview face to face (using a tape recorder or shorthand if you possess this dying skill) as you can glean a lot from meeting an interviewee in person. Alternatively, if geographical location or time restrictions dictate, you can always interview someone by telephone, Skype or even by email, sending them written questions which they then answer in writing.

However, if you are going to conduct an interview in person, here are a few tips on interview technique:

▶ Forewarn your interviewee about how much of their time you are likely to take up in advance of the interview.
▶ On the day, make sure you have contact details for the interviewee in case there is an unforeseen change in your plans and you have to call them en route to the interview.

- ▶ Arrive promptly.
- ▶ Dress appropriately for the occasion and location of the interview.
- ▶ Have all your equipment ready with spare pencil, batteries for voice recorder, etc.
- ▶ Check that your voice recorder is picking up sound adequately before getting stuck into the interview.
- ▶ Initially, talk about how you see the interview unfolding and maybe a little about what you are doing, so as to put the interviewee at ease before launching into the questioning.
- ▶ Be as brief as possible without rushing.
- ▶ Be pre-prepared with open questions (those that require more than a simple yes or no answer) but be relaxed about diverging from your plan if the interviewee leads you off onto a different but relevant subject.
- ▶ Remember to thank them at the end of the interview and ask if you can get back to them if there is anything that you do not understand when you transcribe your recording/notes.

As a freelance writer, it is unfair to promise that the interviewee can see the article or chapter before it goes to press since a sub-editor may alter your copy once it is submitted to a magazine or publisher. However, you can agree to let them check it for accuracy and explain that this may not be the final version of the feature, although direct quotes will not be changed (but may be cut).

Interviewees tend to fall into two distinct categories:

Experts
One of the best ways to have unique and up-to-the minute material for your feature or book is to interview experts within the field. You can contact the press office of professional associations, governing bodies and charities who can put you in touch with an expert, although some press officers may be reluctant to help unless you already have a firm commission.

You can also contact experts directly by contacting research universities or enthusiast clubs and asking if one of the professors, lecturers or experts is willing to be interviewed. It is worth bearing in mind that such experts are extremely busy people so, if they agree to spare the time to talk to you, it is only fair that you have prepared your questions in advance and that you keep the number of questions to an essential minimum.

Case studies

We have already seen that personal stories are a useful tool in the non-fiction writer's arsenal. Ask family and friends if they can furnish you with a story that may be appropriate. Alternatively, some charities and professional associations, particularly in the health arena, have the names of people who are prepared to share their experiences with the press. When using real-life stories, you must always check whether the interviewee wants you to change the name to protect their identity or whether you can use real names. Also, you may have to credit the charity or professional organization which supplied the case study as a matter of courtesy.

Copyright restrictions

During the course of your research, you will collect together a large body of written material on your chosen subject. You can use the ideas expressed in this material to inform your writing but you must not use the exact words as used in the original document. These words are protected by copyright and if you simply repeat them or cut and paste material from the internet into your own feature or book, it is plagiarism.

To avoid copyright infringements, you can contact an author or publisher and ask for permission to reprint a certain section of text. If you supply them with the passage that you would like to use, and commit to crediting the source and acknowledging permission, as long as the extract is not too lengthy, most publishers and authors will agree. Strangely, facts are not covered by copyright so you can copy these at will.

Enough is enough

Once you get into the swing of researching, it can be hard to know when you have enough material. It is a common trap for the novice writer to spend an inordinate amount of time researching as an unconscious way of putting off starting to write. Once you have a good body of research material, switch from research mode to writing mode and get started.

Seeking permissions

In order to reprint copyrighted material in your book, you need to seek permissions, and the sooner you start the better because it can sometimes be a lengthy process.

▶ If you are quoting from a book or article, you will find the name and contact details of the publisher, together with copyright dates, in the opening pages of the book or magazine.

▶ If you want to reprint lyrics from songs, the name of the record company can normally be found on the back cover of CDs, cassettes and records.

Explain in an email or letter about the theme of your book, in what context you would like to use the reprinted material and show the publisher/record company the exact words you will be using. There may be a fee involved but, if used in moderation, many companies are happy for you to reprint as long as you give a full credit.

Once you have a publisher, if you encounter problems tracking down a permission, get the publisher involved. They have legal departments who can find out if something is still in copyright or not, and they may also be able to negotiate a better deal if fees are involved.

INTERVIEW TECHNIQUE EXERCISE

▶ Ask a friend for an interview about his or her hobby (preferably not something that you know much about).
▶ Keep the interview to a maximum of 20 minutes.
▶ Quote parts of the interview in a written profile of the person and their hobby (in circa 750 words).
▶ Show your friend the feature and ask for feedback.

4

Starting to write

In this chapter you will learn:
- *how to get started*
- *how to create readily understandable non-fiction writing*
- *how to grab and keep your reader's attention.*

Where do I start?

Procrastination is the major enemy of the writer. It is too easy to put off starting your book or feature. People often ask how I work at home with all the distractions that entails but, as a professional freelance writer, if I do not produce the goods, I do not get paid. It's a powerful incentive. Perhaps this does not apply directly to you as yet, but even so, self-discipline is still the name of the game if you want to get published. After all, you've done the legwork and collected together the necessary information, quotes and statistics. That was the hard bit. Now is the time to pull it all together and to produce the first draft – this is where the fun starts. If you're still having problems starting, why not try the following tips for curing procrastination:

▶ Set small, achievable goals and promise yourself a reward such as a cup of tea or a biscuit each time a goal is met.
▶ Clear your work area of clutter so that you do not get distracted.
▶ Set yourself a deadline.
▶ Don't be over-ambitious – you're not likely to be able to maintain eight hours a day of solid writing, so don't expect it of yourself.
▶ Keep a log of how many times you've planned to start writing, only to put it off. It's humbling.

- ▶ If there really is no spare time in your day to write, try getting up half an hour earlier.
- ▶ Tell someone you trust about your deadline. That way, they'll give you support and it is an incentive not to let the deadline pass.

Starting to write

There are recognized stages in the writing process. If you follow these stages, taking each step at a time, your writing project will not seem as daunting somehow.

ORDERING

Once you have collected all your material together, you can then plan how you want to join all the component parts together to make a coherent and cohesive whole. How you achieve this depends largely on personal preference. Some writers make a linear plan, putting elements into an order of importance. Others, myself included, prefer to group each piece of research, cuttings and notes into common themes and then work out how you might link these themes so that they follow on from each other. I give each themed group a letter and scribble that letter in red ink on every individual piece of paper/ printout so I can immediately identify in which section of the article/ chapter this information belongs.

Once you have decided on a beginning, middle and end to your feature or chapter, then you will find that your writing moves seamlessly from one theme to the next, from paragraph to paragraph, and the reader is carried fluidly with you through the article.

Insight – the importance of pre-planning

As a writing coach, I am surprised at how often novice writers miss out the important step of giving prior thought to the ordering of their writing. Countless manuscripts arrive that are littered with clumsy phrases, such as 'As I mentioned earlier…'. This is all due to a lack of pre-planning when it comes to structuring articles.

FIRST DRAFT

Even the most experienced writer will confess that starting a book is daunting. If you type 'Chapter one' at the top of a blank page, with the prospect of the whole book stretching before you, it can seem overwhelming and the challenge insurmountable. That is why, when writing a book, I rarely start with the first chapter, as would seem logical. In fact, I start with a chapter that really appeals to me, or one of the shorter chapters. It is a good way to get into the book and to stimulate your writing flow. I then return to the all-important opening chapter at a later date.

That said, there is one word of caution. If you are writing a book, tempting though it may be, do not leave the toughest chapter until the very last moment. Tackle it when you are in the full flow of the writing process and when all is going well.

Irrespective of whether you start at the beginning or at a favoured chapter, the important thing is to get something down on paper. It does not matter if it is not perfect purple prose. Just write whatever comes into your head, and get all your ideas down, as you will have the opportunity to edit and tweak your work at a later stage.

STRUCTURE

Whatever you are writing, be it a book or a magazine article, it should be well structured.

Title You should start with a short, catchy title that grabs the reader's attention. If this is not immediately apparent to you, then at least have a working title in mind so that you know the focus of your work.

Opening paragraphs The purpose of the opening paragraphs of a magazine or newspaper feature is to excite, intrigue or surprise your reader so that he or she is keen to read on. In the same way, the opening paragraphs of each chapter of your book should capture your reader and draw them into the following pages.

Endings Not easy to get right, but if your reader has stayed faithful to you until the end (sadly that's not a given), it is good to finish on a high. Strong endings tend to tie in to the theme of the title or the opening paragraphs so that the reader feels that they have come full circle.

PRESENTATION

When submitting a manuscript to a publishing house or a feature to a magazine or newspaper editor, there are certain industry-wide protocols regarding the presentation of your work that you should adhere to, if possible.

- ▶ Your manuscript should be double-spaced.
- ▶ Paragraphs should be indented (except under a heading).
- ▶ No line breaks after any paragraph, unless you are intending a section break.
- ▶ Quotes in the ordinary text can simply be handled like this: 'Blah, blah, blah.'
- ▶ If you want to include a more extensive quote, then it needs to be indented on both sides, and preferably the line spacing condensed too:

> 'Blah, blah, blah. Blah, blah, blah. Blah, blah, blah. Blah, blah, blah. Blah, blah, blah. Blah, blah, blah. Blah, blah, blah. Blah, blah, blah. Blah, blah, blah. Blah, blah, blah. Blah, blah, blah. Blah, blah, blah. Blah, blah, blah. Blah, blah, blah. Blah, blah, blah. Blah, blah, blah.'

- ▶ Quotes in the text do not need to be italicized.

Writing style

First and foremost, you need to realize that there is no right or wrong style, so do not get too hung up on whether you write well or not. However, the purpose of a non-fiction writer is to convey information in a clear and readily understandable, and preferably, engaging way. In order to do this successfully, there are certain practices that you can adopt when writing that will improve the chances of getting your work published and read.

CONSISTENT VOICE

Whether you choose to write in an informal, conversational style or prefer a more literary, third-person approach is entirely up to you, but whichever you choose, you must stick to it. If you keep changing the voice of the narrator, it will confuse your reader. It's also worth bearing in mind, that even if you opt for a more formal tone, it should still engage the reader.

BE CONCISE

One of the most common mistakes made by the novice non-fiction writer is to use two words where one will do. Whether you feel the need to show a wide vocabulary or simply cannot decide which word to drop, it is a pitfall that you should try to avoid. Aim to be clear, concise and precise wherever possible.

SIMPLE LANGUAGE

Always choose a short, simple word rather than a pretentiously long one (oh, the irony). The aim is to keep your language appropriate to the readership, which does not mean 'dumbing down' or always using short words, but rather keeping the meaning clear and readily understandable.

In the same way, avoid using jargon in your writing unless it is a specialist non-fiction book aimed at a specialist market. Even so, it is useful to put the meaning of a specialized word or phrase in brackets after its first appearance in the text. As a general rule, avoid using specialist jargon in books or articles aimed at the general public.

SHORT SENTENCES AND PARAGRAPHS

A common mistake is to use over-long sentences and paragraphs. This commonly happens when you are trying to explain something complicated and sentences run on out of control. However, it is an easy error to correct as you can usually divide up long sentences and paragraphs using punctuation. For the reader, short sentences help to speed up the pace and conversely, long sentences slow you down. Similarly, short paragraphs help to divide up the text into readily digestible bite-sized chunks making it easier to read and to comprehend.

You should be aiming for an average sentence length of about 15–20 words. Obviously, you can mix in longer and shorter sentences to keep things interesting but err on the side of keeping sentences short, wherever possible. If you work on the principle of one idea in a sentence and one topic per paragraph, this naturally curtails any tendency towards long-winded writing.

DESCRIPTIVE WRITING

By all means use description to bring your writing to life but avoid going overboard on the use of adjectives and adverbs, which can make a sentence flabby (see the exercise at end of this chapter). Most professional non-fiction writers use some description in their writing, albeit subtly. You will find that travel writers in particular draw on all five senses when describing the exotic locations they visit and the unfamiliar foods they sample. This vividly invokes the sights, sounds, smells, tastes and atmosphere of a place for the reader and it is a technique that you can draw on to good effect in your own writing.

STAY ACTIVE

Your work will have more immediacy and be punchier if you use the active tense rather than the passive, wherever possible. So rather than saying, 'The train was stopped by masked men,' you should write, 'Masked men stopped the train.' There will be occasions when the passive voice is required but, in general, stick with the active tense as this is more compelling for the reader.

CLICHÉS

George Orwell's advice to writers is still valid today. He said, 'Never use a metaphor, simile, or other figure of speech which you are used to seeing in print.' Over-used phrases are counter-productive since readers are known to switch off when they come across these hackneyed expressions. Rather than rely on the familiar, why not come up with something original or exciting. If you are unable to find an alternative phrase, simply remove the metaphor or simile from your text.

According to a survey carried out in 2004 by The Plain English Campaign, 'at the end of the day' was voted the most irritating phrase in the English language. Second place in the vote was shared by 'at this moment in time' and the constant use of 'like' as if it were a form of punctuation. 'With all due respect' came fourth. If you know you are guilty of using such phrases and others like them in your writing, then go through it with a red pen and weed out all clichés.

KNOW YOUR READER

It is easy to get so caught up in your writing that you lose sight of who you are aiming your book at. Your book is not for you; it is for a reader who knows less about the subject than you do. So make sure you continually check that you are explaining yourself clearly to your target audience. When writing for the reader, it is often easiest to imagine that you are explaining something to a friend. This keeps the writing concise, focused and accessible.

Insight – say it out loud

If I am not sure if a sentence or paragraph works, I read it out loud like a newsreader. If it is hard to say or to understand when spoken aloud, then I rewrite it and read it out loud again until it sounds sensible.

DON'T PREACH

Although the aim of the non-fiction writer is to convey information to a reader who probably knows less about the subject than yourself, it does not mean that you should take a hectoring or smug tone. Preaching is a sure way to lose your reader before the end of the book, even if you have something useful to say.

CALLING A HALT

For the inexperienced writer, it can be hard to know when to stop writing, as there always seems to be just one more thing to add. However, publishers are generally put off by overly long manuscripts, so unless you want your opus to end up in the rejection pile, it is wise to stick to your chapter breakdown and to resist the temptation to keep adding extra material.

Insight – choose your writing time

Write at the best time of day to suit your nature. If you are an early bird, write for a couple of hours in the morning before the rest of the house awakes. For night owls – definitely my preferred style – you are likely to be more productive in the evening.

Tools for the non-fiction writer

We have seen that writing style is strictly personal and that you will find by trial and error an approach that suits you and suits the kind of book or article that you are writing. Whether you opt for a chatty and relaxed style or prefer the more formal approach, there are certain tricks of the writing trade that you can employ to make your writing more accessible to the reader. Once you become aware of these writing devices, you will start to identify them as you read newspapers, magazines and books, and then you can see how they are used to good effect.

USE QUESTIONS

In magazine journalism, you will often see a question used, frequently to introduce a new idea to the feature and to provoke curiosity. So in its introductory paragraph, a feature on the therapeutic properties of honey in a women's magazine might carry a question along the lines of, 'So is royal jelly the answer to all your health problems?' If you use this technique, you must then make sure that you go on to answer the question in the following paragraphs. It is a useful tool but should not be overused, as this dilutes its impact.

USE HEADINGS

It is rare to see a newspaper or magazine feature or the chapter of a book that does not use headings and sub-headings, and yet you would be surprised at how many sample articles and manuscripts I see that do not contain a single heading. Headings are important as they help to:

▶ signpost a reader through your prose
▶ break up the page, so speeding up the pace
▶ avoid clumsy or abrupt changes in direction in your writing
▶ whet the reader's appetite for what is coming next.

Headings catch the eye and hook readers in, so try to be imaginative when coming up with the wording for headings and sub-headings.

Generally, headings are used to introduce a major theme. Within that section there may well be several components that also deserve to be highlighted, so these are placed under their own secondary heading, known as sub-headings. Occasionally, one of these sub-sections will also be worthy of a heading, and so a sub-subheading or cross-heading is used, and so on. In general, it is wise to keep the number of levels of headings to about three but if sub-headings help to make the point clear to the reader, then use as many as it takes.

In the publishing industry, these levels of headings are designated A-heads, B-heads, C-heads, D-heads and so on, in descending order. They are differentiated by different font sizes and styles according to their importance.

USE STATISTICS

Fact and figures are the bread and butter of the non-fiction writer. You can always support a statement with relevant statistics, which help you to sound authoritative. People are always drawn to the wacky or outlandish, so if you can find some bizarre fact to drop into your copy or a little known statistic, it can be a good tool for keeping the reader's interest. One of my favourite obscure facts that I managed to weave into a feature for *Daily Mail Ski* magazine is that a scientist came up with the formula for happiness and Scottish country dancing was the nearest thing to fulfilling the happiness criteria, with skiing a close second.

Obviously unusual statistics of the 'more people are killed by' variety are always popular – for example coconuts kill more people each year (about 150) than sharks (about 40) – but you can only use this tool once or twice in a feature to best effect. If you put too many statistics in the main body of your text, the reader will get bored and jump ahead. So choose the statistics with the most impact and edit out the rest.

Insight – use reliable sources

If you use facts and statistics in your writing, make sure the source is reliable as editors often ask for provenance, especially from new writers. If using the internet, search governing bodies and professional associations rather than personal opinion websites.

USE BOXED COPY (AKA SIDEBARS)

These are great for breaking up text, varying the pace and for adding emphasis since the eye is naturally drawn to highlighted copy on the page. It is also a useful device for segregating information that does not happily fit in to the main body of the feature/chapter, yet does not warrant a whole sub-section to itself.

USE ANECDOTES AND CASE STUDIES

Anecdotes and case studies are a great way to personalize a feature and to add human interest, which can enliven a serious topic. Naturally, they have to be relevant and should help to reinforce a point you are making or to give additional information. They do not have to be witty and amusing, although it helps.

If you are adding a case study or a personal anecdote, you should have permission to do so. When it comes to adding your own anecdotes, it is best to exercise discretion. Personal anecdotes can build a closer bond between you and your reader if they are appropriate, but you do not want to relate everything back to yourself. If you find yourself writing for popular mass market magazines, you will almost certainly be asked to include case studies and anecdotes in your features.

Editing your work

This is one of the most crucial stages of writing, especially if your first draft has simply been an exercise in getting your thoughts onto paper. It is your chance to tidy up your prose and to sort out any problems with the flow and order of your writing. You should read and re-read your writing before making any amendments but do not start this editing exercise as soon as you have finished writing. Give yourself a break, even leaving it overnight, and come back to it with a fresh eye. This is the only way to judge what you have produced. Once you have read it through a couple of times, you can then start to edit your work. Remember to keep your critical inner-voice in check and do not over-tweak or keep adding new material. Generally, when editing, you are looking to:

▶ Remove repetition (and you can be ruthless in this regard); look for words you may have overused or whether you have repeated an idea/point several times.
▶ Check that your tone and style remain consistent and appropriate to your audience.
▶ Replace any flights of grandiosity with plain English.
▶ Delete anything that is over-familiar or inappropriate.
▶ Rewrite any phrase/section that is clumsy or hard to understand.

PROOFREADING

Once you are happy with your writing, then it is time to proofread your work before submitting it to an editor or publisher. Your aim is to remove all spelling, grammatical or punctuation errors. Unless proofreading is your particular forte, it is a good idea to get someone else to read through looking for these mistakes, as it is sometimes difficult to pick them up from your own work.

Proofreading is an essential part of the writing process because the plain truth is that any publisher or editor who receives an unsolicited manuscript or article that is full of spelling and grammatical mistakes, will simply drop it straight in the slush pile. So always check and double-check your manuscript and remove mistakes before submission, if you want to improve the chances of it being accepted.

If you struggle to find anyone who can help with proofreading, for grammatical guidance, you could turn to Lynn Truss's book *Eats, Shoots and Leaves*, and also Fowler's *Modern English Usage*.

Insight – keep track of your edits
After editing and redrafting your writing, you will end up with various versions of the feature or chapter. Make sure you save each version very carefully with a new file name or include the date in the title – it's so easy to lose track of your amendments otherwise.

DESCRIPTIVE STYLE EXERCISE

Exercise one

You may not realize how much you rely on adjectives and adverbs when you are writing. This exercise cleverly highlights how your writing will improve with the sparing and judicial use of these important descriptive words.

Write a 400-word descriptive piece on any topic you like without using a single adjective. It is surprisingly difficult. Read your writing back out loud – checking to make sure no adjectives have slipped in. Then you can add just one adjective, choosing carefully where to put it to add the maximum emphasis and effect.

Exercise two

Browse through some of your favourite magazines and see if you can spot some of the writers' tools and devices that are outlined in this chapter.

5

Revision and rewriting

In this chapter you will learn:
- *how to assess your own work objectively*
- *how criticism can be constructive*
- *how to rework your writing.*

Let us not confuse revision and rewriting with editing your first draft, which we covered in the previous chapter. Revision and rewriting is the next phase of the process and it can only take place once you have a copy of the first draft that you are roughly happy with, and a certain amount of time has elapsed.

The revision process

The revision process is perhaps one of the most protracted phases of writing, but it is a necessary one. The final version of your writing will benefit enormously from an objective review from yourself and others.

YOUR INPUT

You need a decent break between finishing the first draft and revising your work. Whether you leave it a week or several months before returning to your manuscript, this period of distancing is essential in order for you to become objective. When you finally return to your work, do not start with a red pen in hand. Rather, print out your manuscript and read it through completely, in one go, just as a prospective reader would do. Then when you have finished, you can finally note down your general first reactions, as objectively as you can.

Once you have completed this exercise, you can then re-read it with a critical eye (and a red pen if you like), putting notes in the margin as you go about what works and what does not; what needs amending and what needs moving or omitting. Do not let your inner self-critic run away with you. The whole point of this exercise is to remain as objective and as impartial as possible.

GETTING HELP

At this point of the revision exercise, it is a good idea to get feedback from others. Although you are probably shuddering at the mere thought of showing your work to anyone else, realistically, you will have to reveal it to the outside world at some point. However, you are not alone in feeling protective of your manuscript. Many writers liken sharing their text to 'baring their soul' or 'revealing their most intimate self to scrutiny'. I particularly like the way Paulo Coelho describes it when he says, 'Writing books is a socially acceptable form of getting naked in public.'

Nonetheless, getting feedback from friends, family, and trusted others is of great value. Principally, you are asking them to check for comprehension – does it make sense to the reader? If they have feedback on style and structure, so much the better, as long as you can count on them to be honest and to have your best interests at heart. So choose wisely.

Loved ones

Writers often turn firstly to family and friends for review. This is often a good idea but bear in mind that your partner or a parent may find it impossible to give you impartial advice for fear of hurting your feelings. For this reason, it is sometimes better to look for someone slightly more removed.

By contrast, there are some writers who find that their nearest and dearest are not at all supportive of their writing endeavours. For whatever reason, if you experience reactions from those closest to you varying from condescension ('It's nice that she has an interest') to actual hostility ('Why would anyone want to read something that you've written?') then these individuals have effectively ruled themselves out of a reviewing role. As a general rule of thumb, avoid discussing your writing with negative people and limit its exposure to those who support you or who can be positive and constructive in their criticism. You will almost certainly have someone in your circle of friends or acquaintances who fits the bill perfectly and who would be only too happy to review your writing.

When calling in a favour like this, I find that it is most useful and time effective if you ask the reviewer to mark up your manuscript as they read, rather than simply giving you an overview of their general feelings. In this way, you get their immediate and detailed response to your work, which is generally much more instructive than generalities. Why not suggest that they put notes in the margin along the lines of:

- ▶ awkward
- ▶ too long
- ▶ out of place
- ▶ needs more explanation
- ▶ not relevant
- ▶ good.

At the same time, there is a double benefit if they can also annotate in the margin any spelling and grammar mistakes or any jargon that they come across, which you may have missed.

Insight – have reasonable expectations

Although it is reasonable to hope for support and respect for your writing from your friends and family, it does not mean they have to be as excited and involved in it as you are. Remember, it's your passion not theirs. So be reasonable in your expectations of loved ones if you want to save yourself from disappointment.

Experts

If you are writing a specialist non-fiction book, it can be helpful to get it peer reviewed by an expert in the field. Perhaps you have a fellow enthusiast who could cast an eye over your writing and give you feedback on its accuracy, contemporaneousness or if there are any obvious omissions. Alternatively, you could contact a specialist that you do not know personally by email and letter and ask if they would be willing to peer review a specific chapter that is relevant to their field of expertise. Many specialists are only too happy to check features or chapters for technical accuracy, especially if they are quoted in the text.

If you decide to involve a specialist, it may be preferable to send them a more polished version for consideration – perhaps a second or third draft. It is then customary to mention their assistance in the acknowledgements when your book is published.

Structured support

Some writers prefer to turn to others who share an interest or have expertise in writing rather than to those who know them. This can be an effective way to get feedback on something specific that you have written, or simply to get tips and ideas on how to go about the revision and rewriting process if you hit a wall. I should point out though that other writers may not be able to resist the temptation of telling you how they would have done things differently. This is not particularly constructive. Remember, you simply want advice on how to improve your manuscript. To find your nearest writing support, check out your local directory, go online or refer to the resources listed in Taking it further. Why not consider:

▶ **Joining a writing circle** Good for encouragement, inspiration and genuine criticism from like-minded individuals. Be wary of groups that are nothing more than glorified social gatherings though. If that's the case, find another group.
▶ **Attending writing classes, workshops or courses** Ranging from local education classes through weekend workshops to overseas residential courses in exotic locations. Courses also range enormously in price but there is something to suit every pocket. Such classes/courses can be helpful for focusing your intention, polishing your writing skills and many are wonderfully inspirational too.
▶ **Visiting writing-related websites** If you want to reach a broader circle of people with similar interests, then there are plenty of writing-related websites where you can chat about shared problems and solutions with countless other writing enthusiasts in the online forums. Some sites also post topical podcasts, which you can listen to at your leisure.
▶ **Paying for professional services** People think nothing of turning to a personal trainer to help them to get fit so why not consider seeking the services of a professional writing coach or editor? If you have exhausted local or online support, a reputable editor should be able to help you to rewrite your manuscript so that it turns out as you envisaged. Make sure they are clear with you from the start about fees involved, what they can do for you and how long it should take.

Rewriting tips

Once you have the feedback from your reviewers, you can add their comments to your own so that you start to form an overview of what needs to be done to improve your manuscript. Writers often omit to include the good feedback, feeling a natural embarrassment, but if you know what you have done well, then you can repeat this style/technique elsewhere.

I suggest that you group the comments into categories such as style, structure, omissions and so on, as this helps you to assimilate and correlate the feedback. In this way, you can see if a pattern is emerging. For example, you may find that there is a consensus that there is a problem with ordering in a certain chapter. In this case, you can look at it more closely to see if material should appear earlier or later in the chapter, or whether it belongs in a different chapter entirely. Once you have your overview, you can revisit your original outline for the book. Have you deviated from your original plan? If you have adhered to it, does it work or not? If necessary, you may decide to rewrite your outline.

Now you can finally turn your attention to rewriting or reorganizing the sections that need attention. As you redraft, bear in mind that your amendments may have a knock-on effect that will require you to make adjustments to text elsewhere. For example, if you have a cross-reference in one chapter to material in another chapter, and that material has now moved, you will naturally have to alter the original cross-reference accordingly.

Insight – trust yourself

When you review the feedback, you may have received conflicting views on what is required. These comments are essentially others' opinions and not necessarily right or wrong. Ultimately, trust your own gut reaction and go with what best resonates with you.

Rewriting is sometimes the stage where inexperienced writers hit a wall. Often they realize that something needs to change but they cannot see exactly how to go about making the amendments. At this point, it is easy to either become obsessive or to let the project languish. If you get stuck, and a solution is not immediately obvious to you, move on to another area of the manuscript that also needs attention. Once you have fixed that, you can return to the thorny problem a little later and with a success under your belt, you will probably find an answer is staring you in the face.

It is usually a good idea to concentrate on one chapter at a time, otherwise the number of corrections and general rewriting can appear insurmountable. Attack the job in bite-sized chunks and it will seem less daunting.

The one thing that it is crucial to remember is that a rewrite is not an exercise in adding new material. Unless there is a recent development that demands inclusion or the review exercise has identified a hole in your project, you should be reworking the manuscript, not adding to it. If anything, you can use the rewriting exercise as another opportunity to pare down any repetitions or unnecessary copy that you missed on the first edit. Since the most common criticism levelled by publishers at unsolicited manuscripts from non-fiction writers is that they are way too long, you should take any opportunity to reassess whether your material is substantive or puffery.

In truth, when pared back to the essentials, some book ideas are probably better suited to magazine articles. At this point, it is better to be honest with yourself and to rework a manuscript into a feature than to send off an overly long text to a publisher only to receive a string of rejections.

When you rewrite, you should always be asking yourself whether your text adheres to the following writing rules:

- ▶ Does it make sense?
- ▶ Is it in the right order?
- ▶ Does it stay on track throughout the chapter/feature without deviating off on odd tangents?
- ▶ Can I condense the number of sentences in this paragraph or the number of words in this sentence?

REVIEWING EXERCISES

Exercise one

Why not make yourself a checklist? Then go through your feature or each chapter of your manuscript and check it against your list. Here are some suggestions for your checklist, but you can add more that are appropriate to your specific writing.

Meaning
▶ Does it make sense?
▶ Have I explained all technical/specialist phrases or unfamiliar concepts?
▶ Is the theme of the chapter or feature clear and do I stay on track?

Accuracy
▶ Have I double-checked all the facts, dates and statistics?
▶ Are the quotations accurate and accredited?
▶ Have the case studies been approved?

Ordering
▶ Does the material run in the right order or does a section need to move further forward (giving it greater priority) or further back?
▶ Would some material be better collected together in a box or sub-section rather than scattered throughout the text?

Layout
▶ Are the headings and sub-headings in a uniform style?
▶ Are the headings relevant?
▶ Does each chapter have a general introduction before moving into the main discussion of ideas?

Style
▶ Are there any phrases or sentences that sound clumsy?
▶ Can I condense any sections, paragraphs or sentences that are overly long?
▶ Have I eliminated all repetition?
▶ Is the tone appropriate – too patronizing or too informal?
▶ Do I address the reader directly?
▶ Is there energy in my writing – will a reader stick with it?

Exercise two

If you find it hard to review your own work objectively, take a look at someone else's writing and critique that. Practise on as many manuscripts as possible, then return to your own and apply the critiquing techniques that you have newly acquired on your own writing.

6

Writing self-help and 'how to' books

In this chapter you will learn:
- *how to perfect the right tone*
- *how to share your knowledge and information*
- *how to introduce devices to maintain reader interest*.

This is one of the most promising genres for the newcomer to non-fiction writing. It is a growing market and publishers are optimistic, buoyed by an apparently inexhaustible audience of readers looking to:

▶ increase their specialist knowledge
▶ bolster personal, social or professional skills
▶ resolve personal issues.

Although publishers are always looking for new ideas, equally, they are also seeking a new twist or different approach to existing subjects. So you do not have to reinvent the wheel with self-help or 'how to' books; you simply have to have an innovative approach to a familiar but perennially popular subject.

There is also a high demand for 'how to' features in specialist, hobbyist and women's consumer magazines. If you are an authority in a specific field or hobby, then magazine articles could be a good place to start your writing career. And, while the money may not be enough to retire on, it can be a steady income for a specialist writer, since editors are obliged to fill pages on the same topic month after month, so creating a high demand for new material.

Effectively sharing knowledge

Although self-help and 'how to' books serve a similar function, namely to give readers new abilities, they are subtly different. A self-help book focuses on routes to personal development and self-enlightenment and shows ways to overcome perceived or existing problems. Whereas the sole purpose of a 'how to' book is to help the reader to acquire specific skills.

Nonetheless, the way you compile self-help and 'how to' books and the tools you use in the writing of them share many of the same basic principles. For example, both genres are always practical, often use step-by-step procedures, and frequently are illustrated. All are designed to make the information they present as easy to understand as possible.

One of the downsides to these practical books is that they often require specially commissioned illustrations or original photography to accompany the step-by-step exercises. This increases the production cost of the book, especially if it involves colour printing, and this can make the price of some self-help or 'how to' publishing projects prohibitive. Nonetheless, if you are pitching a proposal for a book that is heavily practical participation/exercise based, then you can point out that many or most of the procedures are self-explanatory and will not require illustration. Of course, if you do this, you must make sure that your instructions are completely clear and easy to follow. To this end, it is worth getting someone to actually follow the instructions to highlight any areas that are not explicit enough.

When giving thought to how you might compile your specialist knowledge into a 'how to' or self-help book, bear in mind that these books tend to fall into two main categories, so helping you to decide upon a suitable chapter breakdown.

STEP-BY-STEP BOOK

Do you have a specific programme for solving a problem that perhaps involves progressively learning new skills? Or can you explain how the reader should develop skills by following an evolutionary process of steps? Each stage or step naturally lends itself to forming a chapter of the book. This progressive style is particularly effective for 'how to' books but can also be used for books on DIY, self-improvement, fitness, sports, diet and health to good effect.

MODULAR BOOK

When the content of your book can be broken down into clear component parts, which together give the reader a new skill or solve a problem, then you are probably looking at a modular book. Basically, each component part takes a chapter of the book. So, the main components of my book on *Getting Your Kids Active* comprised:

▶ developing a positive mental approach
▶ making time to get active
▶ motivating your child
▶ developing a good food attitude
▶ encouraging couch-potatoes and bigger (overweight) kids
▶ staying the course.

Naturally, these components each form a separate chapter in the book and the overall manuscript then becomes a comprehensive self-help guide for parents who want to get their kids to do more exercise, sport or physical activity.

Insight – recovery books

There is a third type of self-help book that is aimed at readers wanting to recover from addictive or compulsive behaviours. These usually follow the classic 12-, 10- or 7-step programmes, as typified by Alcoholics Anonymous. However, unless you are a specialist in assisting this sort of recovery, I would suggest you consider one of the other genres first.

Accessible style

There are a few universal stylistic rules that apply to writing self-help and 'how to' books. If you employ the following writing techniques, you will ensure your manuscript has just the right reassuring and sympathetic, yet authoritative style.

STAY INFORMAL

When writing this genre of book, you should make sure that you use an informal, conversational tone. You do not want to be too correct or text book in your approach, as the aim is to put your reader at ease. Try to cultivate a style that is akin to explaining to a friend how to do something. Just as you would in a conversation, you talk directly to your reader using the 'you' form in your writing. Occasionally, there will be sentences where this is not possible but in general, addressing your reader directly builds a bond of trust between you that is important if they are going to follow your advice with confidence.

BE SYMPATHETIC

You are aiming to be sympathetic to your reader. You want them to know that you are on their side and that you are in this together. So, avoid preaching or being critical – remember: it is just as if you were coaching a friend. In this way, the tone automatically becomes supportive, reassuring and optimistic – the perfect recipe for a self-help or 'how to' book.

KEEP IT SIMPLE

You may have to use the occasional technical or specialist term (if so, make sure you give an explanation of its meaning the first time it appears), but generally speaking, you want to keep the language simple and to use everyday phrases.

KNOW YOUR READER

If you are writing a book on pregnancy, you can be pretty well assured that your reader is female, so you are then at liberty to address your reader as 'her' throughout the book. However, if you are not so sure of the profile of your readership, then it is best to be as gender-balanced as possible. Unfortunately, this can lead to some clumsy sentences but your choices are grammatically limited. Either write both 'he or she' and 'women and men' or you can interchange 'he' and 'she' in alternating chapters. The only other option available is to full back on the 'they' and 'them' solution, which can jar on the ear rather. However, do not get too hung up on this – it is a thorny issue that has vexed writers for generations, but any of these three approaches is acceptable to a publisher. If you decide to use one pronoun throughout the book, then state so in your introduction and then it should not give offence.

Writing tools used in self-help and 'how to' books

Seasoned writers who specialize in self-help and 'how to' books have a collection of writing tools at their disposal aimed at keeping the reader's attention and clarifying points that are being made. If you take any book from this genre from your bookshelves you will see many of the following devices used throughout.

CASE STUDIES

Both case histories and anecdotal stories are always popular, in self-help books in particular, because they reassure the reader that they are not alone; that there are other ordinary people like them who share their predicament, problem or situation. Case studies and anecdotes are especially useful when they have a positive outcome, since these are uplifting and inspirational as well as conveying a constructive message. You can use a case history or an anecdote whenever you want to reinforce the point that you are making in the body text. Wherever possible:

▶ keep both types of account relatively brief and to the point
▶ change the identities of individuals and locations so they cannot be identified, if desired
▶ make them positive, inspiring and motivational
▶ keep anecdotes about yourself to a reasonable level
▶ personalize the account, e.g. use a name (even if it is fictional) rather than say 'a friend of mine' and give a brief description of them.

TEAM SPIRIT

Posing a series of questions along the lines of 'Do you find yourself...?' or 'Have you ever...?' followed by a list of hypothetical common experiences forms a bond with your reader as they realize that not only do you have knowledge of their situation but you also have empathy. This immediately produces a team spirit that helps the reader to have confidence in you, the writer. The questions can take a bulleted list form. So in a feature on post-natal depression, you might find something along these lines:

'It may be time to seek professional help if, as a new mother, you start to feel:

▶ increasingly despondent and hopeless
▶ permanently listless
▶ unable to cope with household chores or the care of the baby
▶ anxious, often over own health or health of baby
▶ tense and/or panicky
▶ disorganized and lacking in concentration
▶ so anxious you experience difficulty in sleeping
▶ a reluctance to bathe, get dressed or do your make-up
▶ a loss of interest in sex
▶ isolated.'

As readers identify with some or all of the statements, so they feel safe in your hands and reassured that you can help them.

Alternatively, you can introduce the series of common and probably shared experiences in the body text, with or without the question format. For example, in the introduction of my book *You and Your Ageing Parents: How to Balance Your Needs and Theirs*, I used this technique as follows:

> **Spending time with your parents once you are an independent adult can be wonderfully rewarding, but it can also be fraught with difficulties. You may have unresolved issues from your own childhood to address. You may find that seeing a loved one diminishing before your eyes is too hard to handle. Or you may simply not get on very well with your mother or father.**
>
> **Whatever your particular circumstances, you can benefit from sharing the ideas contained in this book and take comfort in knowing that you are not alone – others are undergoing similar experiences throughout the UK. In fact, in April 2001, 5.2 million people were providing unpaid care in England and Wales – that's 13 per cent of those between the ages of 16–74; and, more particularly, this is 1 in 5 people in their 50s.**

As you can see, a reader can identify with the theoretical situations outlined. The point is then reinforced by the statistics, which clearly show that most people who find themselves in 'the sandwich' position (caring for kids and ageing parents) are women in their 40s and 50s, who are the target audience for the book.

STATISTICS AND FACTS

In the above scenario, statistics were used to support a point that I was making to show commonality with the reader. However, bold or startling facts and figures about the topic can also be used to good effect to capture the reader's attention and to introduce drama into a subject that may not be that exciting.

HEADINGS AND SUB-HEADINGS

Good use of headings and sub-headings is important in all genres of non-fiction writing but especially so for 'how to' or self-help books where the reader may be hopping among the relevant sections of interest rather than reading chapters successively.

Headings effectively help to signpost the reader through the chapter. If you use a heading or sub-heading at the beginning of each key change of subject or above a major theme, a reader can effortlessly locate the section they want. If you use an exciting or clever heading, you are even more likely to make them want to read on. Headings can be functional but should never be dull. Wherever possible, headings should be:

▶ exciting
▶ enticing
▶ witty
▶ dramatic
▶ stimulating
▶ intriguing
▶ promissory
▶ snappy.

All of the above qualities have the effect of luring the reader in and making them eager to read on. If you hold out a promise of benefit as well, then you will have the reader hooked. This style of heading is particularly well utilized in slimming magazines where you routinely see headings such as 'Lose a stone in just four weeks'.

Avoid using technical or academic terms as headings. Apart from the fact that technical terms are off-putting, especially if you are new to the subject, they are not helpful to those looking for support or new skills. So the heading 'Kinesics' should be replaced with 'Interpreting Body Language'.

Insight – keep it positive

I find that negative headings put people off, so keep the tone positive. Even if the section is about the dangers of fatty foods, the spin on the heading could be 'Six of the best ways to lower cholesterol'.

LISTS

A list is a great way to condense material and to present a series of important ideas. Lists are also visually arresting, so not only do they break up large swathes of text, but they also draw the reader's eye to that section. If you find that important information or ideas are getting buried in the dense body of main text, pull them out into a bulleted or asterisked list. In general, numbered lists should be avoided as these imply some sort of sequential pecking order.

Rather, numbered lists should be reserved for instructions for exercises in self-help or 'how to' books.

PARTICIPATION

It is the practical aspect of reader participation that sets self-help and 'how to' books apart from other kinds of non-fiction writing. When readers are actively involved, they interact with the book and this empowers them to feel that they are taking positive steps towards change or towards gaining greater skills. Participation strengthens the reader's confidence in their ability and may actually solve problems or give them the increased expertise they seek. There are many different ways to encourage the reader to participate, and you can incorporate as many or as few of the following techniques as you like into your book:

Exercises These usually take the form of numbered instructions that lead the reader step-by-step through the process of an activity that can range from DIY and crafts, through sports, exercises and weight loss, to improving emotional and spiritual wellbeing.

Quizzes These can take many forms including multiple choice, boxes to tick, 'True or false' and points awarded to add up, but the purpose of all of them is to make sure your reader remembers key points and to put them on the path to inner enlightenment and self-discovery. It is up to you how challenging you make your quiz – obviously it should be appropriate to the target readership so a quiz in a children's book should not contain degree standard questions – but make sure it is engaging and, where possible, fun.

Checklists These take the form of a list where each entry is preceded by an empty box that the reader can tick. Most useful when you want to help the reader to remember a series of important ideas, to make sure they have included every element of a process or system, or to come to a decision about something. Sometimes it is helpful to leave some blank lines at the bottom of a checklist so that the reader can add notes and observations that may be illuminating for them, perhaps making them more aware of how they think, feel and act.

Comparison tables Usually in the form of two columns, occasionally more, a comparison table is where you compare and contrast the items in one column with those in the next. You will probably have seen it in the form of a 'Pros and cons' list but they can be used to compare just about anything from effective and ineffective line management techniques to 'True *vs* false' or 'Boys *vs* girls'.

Guidelines This is a useful device when you want to give advice on any topic, for example: 'Things to avoid', 'Things to include', 'How to improve a skill' – the list is endless. This form of guidance needs to be concise and can be a summary of more detailed information contained in the body of the chapter.

Visualization Leading the reader through a visualization exercise helps to build confidence and skill. It is a technique that is widely used in the sports arena at the highest levels since it has been proven that mentally picturing a course of action and an outcome can enhance performance and produce physical and psychological changes. Inviting the reader to undertake a visualization exercise has traditionally been the preserve of emotional, mental and spiritual development, business rehearsal and sporting books, but it has many other far-reaching applications.

If you are going to employ any of the participation techniques listed, it is worth bearing in mind that you need to explain clearly to the reader how to do it and what they are likely to get out of it. In addition, if the participation involves giving answers, you must also help the reader to be able to evaluate their results. If not, the reader will be left feeling flat and alone, which is counter-productive.

READER PARTICIPATION EXERCISES

Exercise one

I was once invited to write an outdoor survival book aimed at 11- to 14-year-old boys under my pen name, Rory Storm. It was full of practical step-by-step procedures for lighting fires, making shelters and finding your way using a stick. For each exercise, I would write the instructions and then invite my son and one of his friends to work through the procedure following the equipment list and instructions. If they produced an acceptable 'services-style pot-hanger,' for example, it went in. If the exercise failed due to lack of clarity, I rewrote it. It proved great fun for the boys, and a salutary lesson in instruction writing for me.

▶ Choose a specialist skill that you possess and write a set of step-by-step instructions (aimed at a novice) to complete a task. For example, if you are a knitter, you could explain how to cast on a row of stitches and knit a row of pearl and a row of plain knitting.

▶ If you prefer, you can choose an everyday household chore and explain that in a step-by-step fashion.

▶ When you are happy with your set of instructions, ask a volunteer to follow them to the letter (without using any of their own knowledge) to see if they work effectively.

Exercise two

▶ Write a multiple-choice quiz on your chosen topic and create a marking scheme too.

▶ Add some humour to your quiz if possible.

You can have a lot of fun with this. Here is an excerpt from the introductory quiz that appeared in the survival book I mentioned in exercise one above. It gives you an idea of what I have in mind.

Example quiz

1 Your car gets a flat tyre, veers off the road and crashes in the middle of the desert. You're the only survivor. Should you:
   a Wait by the vehicle wreckage for help?
   b Set off walking to get help?
   c Try and repair the car?

2 Most accidents in the hills happen:
   a Between 7 a.m. and 9 a.m.
   b Between 2 p.m. and 4 p.m.
   c Between 10 p.m. and midnight.

3 You find yourself in open country in a heavy thunderstorm. Where is the best place to seek shelter?
   a In the lee of a rock
   b Under a tree
   c In a storm drain

4 What is the best method of lighting a fire in the wild?
   a Gasolene/petrol
   b Flame-thrower
   c Tinder and match

Answers

Shall we see how you got on? Award yourself 3 points for every correct answer.

1a It is much easier for a rescue party to find a large wreckage area than to find a small individual in the vastness of the desert. You can also use the vehicle for shelter in the cold desert nights. Unless you're a qualified mechanic, I don't reckon your chances are very high of getting a crashed vehicle back on the road again, do you?

2b Most people have accidents on the way back from an adventure in the hills. By the end of a day's walking, they are often tired and not as careful as they are earlier in the day while still fresh. Unless they have been lost on the hill or delayed for some reason, very few walkers are mad enough to still be out in the hills at night. It's sheer number crunching that dictates that there are fewer accidents at night.

3a Head for the rock every time. If you shelter under a tree you're asking to get struck by lightning. If you chose 3c, just think about it for a minute. What's a storm drain for? Yes, to divert excessive rainfall. So what's likely to come rushing down your cosy hideaway? You got it – a torrent of devastating water. NEVER go near storm drains.

4c Tinder and match is far and away the best and safest way to light a fire in the open. Gasolene or petrol is highly flammable and extremely dangerous – if you have absolutely no alternative (and I strongly recommend that you never touch it – leave it to an adult and they should exercise extreme care too), carefully soak a rag and light this. Never ever pour petrol directly onto a fire unless you want to go up in flames. A flame-thrower is just a mite excessive, wouldn't you agree? If you chose this answer, you're obviously the sort of guy who uses a hammer to crack an egg!

Scoring

So, was it harder than you thought or did you find it a cinch? Whatever your score, there's always plenty more to learn in the field of survival. I've been out there practising survival skills most of my life and I'm still discovering new tips and techniques.

0–4 points: Oh dear me. Not such a great score but the only way to look at it is that you've got plenty of room for improvement. I hope to goodness you're scoring better by the end of this book though, or I won't be coming on any adventures with you!

4–8 points: Well, that's more like it. You've obviously got a grasp of the basics but could do with honing your skills and picking up a few more tricks of the trade.

8–12 points: Well done. You've certainly been paying attention at scout camp. But never rest on your laurels (unless there's nothing else to sleep on!) because there are plenty more survival tips to pick up.

Whatever your score, I think it's time to roll up our sleeves and get down to the dirty business of surviving, don't you?

7

Writing creative non-fiction

In this chapter you will learn:
- *what creative non-fiction is*
- *when to use creative non-fiction*
- *how to find a subject*
- *how to research your book/feature.*

What is creative non-fiction?

This is a relatively new genre of writing that combines the use of literary craft with factually accurate prose about real people and real events. So rather than traditional non-fiction writing, scholarship or journalism where information, events and facts are reported in an unembellished and straightforward way, the creative non-fiction writer uses description and story telling to make the ideas and information more inviting, compelling and accessible.

Although in the past there has been controversy about the legitimacy of creative non-fiction as a genre (and even as a term), it is a style of writing that has become increasingly popular with the public and it seems it is here to stay. The term was coined in the early 1980s, but in fact this style of writing has been around very much longer. In the 1960s, it was called 'literary journalism' or 'new journalism.' At the time, author Tom Wolfe who wrote the creative non-fiction classic, *The Right Stuff*, believed it 'would wipe out the novel as literature's main event'.

However, if you read classics such as Ernest Hemingway's *Death in the Afternoon* or George Orwell's *Down and Out in Paris and London*, you will see that the dramatic reportage style of creative non-fiction writing has been represented in the literary world for many years.

HOW IS IT NOW USED?

Creative non-fiction writing can be applied to almost any style of non-fiction writing but it is most commonly found in the field of memoir, autobiography, biography, historical and travel writing.

Far and away, the biggest growth in creative non-fiction in recent years has been in the area of historical books, as witnessed by the runaway success of Hilary Mantel's *Wolf Hall*, a dramatized account of the life of Thomas Cromwell that vividly invokes life in Tudor England. Published in April 2009, *Wolf Hall* became the most popular Man Booker Prize-winner to date, with sales of 137,150 in hardback in the six months after the win was announced in October 2009. Yet, not everyone is pleased by the new popularity of the genre. Although not speaking specifically about *Wolf Hall*, Antony Beevor, the historian and bestselling author of *Stalingrad*, is reported to deplore what he calls 'histo-tainment' and 'faction-creep'.

Nonetheless, despite the reservations of some purists, creative non-fiction is proving immensely popular with the public and with publishers. So although it requires more research than a pure fiction novel and more imaginative input than a straightforward non-fiction book, you may well consider that it is worth the extra effort in order to create an engaging book. Certainly, publishers are keen to replicate the success of *Wolf Hall*, and magazine editors are looking to enliven their travel pages with good creative travel features (see Chapter 11), so there is undoubtedly a growing market out there for the creative non-fiction writer.

Choosing a subject

You may already have a topic or person in mind. Is there a member of the family who lived through the dramatic events of World War II, for example, whose personal story you would like to bring to life? Perhaps you have your own story to tell, or there is a person from history who is not well known but who has a life that could be of interest to the public? Is there a figure from the past that you admire and would like to bring to life for others to enjoy? Often the inspiration for creative non-fiction biography or memoir writing lies closer to home. If you talk to older relatives, there are often family legends that are passed down verbally through the generations. Perhaps an ancestor had a dramatic life that is worth exploring in greater depth?

Insight – my family memoir

Everyone in my family knows that my great-grandmother was disowned by her wealthy family after running away with the ornamental stone mason who worked in the grounds, but this is purely oral history. So I took the precaution of interviewing all of my elderly relatives who had heard the story first-hand as children so that one day, I can check marriage certificates and so on at the relevant records office with a view to writing her story.

If travel is the area of creative non-fiction that you would like to explore, you can draw on your own experiences or again, those of your relatives and friends. In your descriptions of a trip to Tunisia, for example, you could juxtapose your vivid descriptions of modern Tunisian life in the beach resorts and cities with your imaginings of life in the ancient Carthaginian Empire, prompted by your visits to the ruined amphitheatres and dwellings.

Researching your project

Without wishing to bang on about this too much, thorough research is essential for successful creative non-fiction. The good news is that there are now so many great sources to choose from which can make a research-based project so much easier. Here are a few that I have used over the years.

RELATIVES, FRIENDS AND COLLEAGUES

Start with those closest to you and work out from there. If you are writing an autobiography close family members and friends should be able to shed light on your childhood experiences or may have photos, newspaper clippings or oral stories if it is a biography of someone in the family line. Next, you can speak to teachers, colleagues, club mates and so on. Spread the word about what you are doing and you will be surprised how the news travels and invariably someone comes out of the blue with some useful information. If people are not able to furnish details on your chosen subject, they may well have ideas that could save you time if they have been involved in a similar project, for example. So do not discount any leads without looking into them, albeit that many if not most will be a dead end.

THE INTERNET

The web has become an invaluable research tool for the creative non-fiction writer and much of the investigative legwork can be done from the comfort of your own home. Obviously, it is important to exercise caution if you are using a source that is not well known or familiar to you, since there are so many bogus, misguided or even ill-intentioned sites masquerading as authoritative sources but you will soon develop a sense of what is worth reading and what should be skipped.

If you are writing a biography or memoir, the online census returns and other genealogy and biography sites are invaluable (see Taking it further for more details).

LIBRARIES

National and local libraries are a remarkable resource for researchers and, in my experience librarians are usually keen to help. Whether it is scrolling through back issues of newspapers or tracking down a useful reference book, ask the staff to assist you if you have problems, as they are highly trained and generally experienced and know all the short cuts.

RECORDS OFFICES

Depending on the nature of your topic, you could look for valuable background information contained in the records of schools, churches and local authorities, as well as valuation rolls, welfare records or electoral registers. This can provide a wide range of biographical detail that puts the life of your chosen subject into context.

Compiling your notes

You will be amazed at just how much material you gather as you go about researching your project. Then comes the tricky task of sorting through the mass of facts, interviews, news clippings and snippets of information that you have collected and deciding what is worth including and what can be discarded.

For the novice writer, deciding what survives the cull and what goes in the reject pile is one of the hardest tasks, since it is only natural to want to include everything that you have discovered. Nonetheless, it is important that you choose only the salient information that will help you to bring the story to life for the reader. If your story is littered with too much detail, you will lose the reader's attention and goodwill. Once the cull has been made, you are then able to organize the surviving information, make an outline, and get started on your creative non-fiction project.

Insight – taking notes

When compiling my material, I read long documents, make my own abridged notes and keep them in the 'to use' pile while filing the original. In this way, I have the information I need at my fingertips but I don't have to cart heavy files around with me.

Writing good creative non-fiction

The key to good creative non-fiction writing lies in the preparation. You must research your project thoroughly. This may mean trawling the internet, visiting your local library or public records office, performing interviews, visiting locations and taking copious notes. These notes should not only cover what happens but also what you see, hear, smell, taste and touch at the time, so you can draw on these senses when you come to write it up at a later date.

Once you have compiled all the background necessary for your book, you can then start thinking about how you can incorporate the literary elements of theme, setting, characters, points of view and dialogue into the non-fiction narrative. In this way, you can bring any story, account or situation alive. Give some thought to the following strategies, which can help you to develop a creative story.

STRUCTURE

Whether you are writing a biography, history or travel feature/book, it does not have to be a chronology of events. By that I mean you do not have to start at the very beginning and follow a timeline through to the very end. You can start anywhere on the journey. Why not choose a startling or memorable event that will pull the reader into the story straightaway?

ACCURACY

Remember this is still non-fiction so you should not make up facts. If you are in doubt, use the words 'perhaps' or 'maybe' to preface a possible but not certain occurrence. Then you can use your imagination to develop the creative story around the facts. If you are going to include quotes, then you will need to tape record your interviews/conversations in order to ensure accuracy. If you find useful and relevant information in old or legal documents, you can quote directly as the archaic and specialized language lends authenticity and gravitas to your project, and can be intriguing to the reader.

Staying on the right side of the law

Since creative non-fiction is dealing with facts, albeit in a literary way, there is a good chance that you will be quoting from the reference books and official documents that you have used for your research. If this is the case, you must be mindful of copyright infringement, getting permissions and including acknowledgments.

If you plan to quote chunks of another author's writing, then you will need permission from the copyright holder – usually the author or publisher – and a fee will possibly be charged. Even if the author is dead, the copyright continues for a further 75 years and you would have to contact his estate for permissions.

In biography writing, it is not unusual to reproduce correspondence or legal documents but, yet again, copyright is applicable and is vested in the writer of the letters. It is no good asking your granny if you can reproduce the letters that she received from her lover in the First World War, as she does not hold the copyright. That belongs to the lover (or his successors) and it is he that you must ask – and I recommend that you get all permissions in writing. You are also obliged to seek and pay for permissions from the relevant authorities if you reproduce birth or marriage certificates.

And finally, once you have sorted out all copyright issues, you must make sure that all sources for quotations and documents are properly credited. This whole long-winded process may sound tiresome but I'm afraid it is essential if you want to keep your writing legal – and any potential publisher will expect nothing less.

POINT OF VIEW

There are two sides to every story, so the old adage says, and although it may be a cliché, it is worth bearing in mind when writing creative non-fiction. No one wants to hear only the positives, triumphs and successes of someone's life. Biography and memoir writing is now very much 'warts and all'. Try to write about yourself, your subject or the destination (if travel writing) from different viewpoints.

CHARACTERS AND SETTINGS

Fiction writers are often told to write a biography of their fictional characters so that they know them inside out. For creative non-fiction, you are turning this principle on its head; the character is real but you have to describe them to your reader in such a way that they leap off the page and they can easily picture them. To do this, you do not have to be too overt and blurt out a lengthy account of height, weight, eye colour and features. Rather, you can reveal the character by degrees and subtly. Try to avoid obvious and over-used adjectives such as 'tall', 'pretty', 'plump' and so on, and go for something more telling and specific to that person.

You can also describe their actions to give insight into their personality. I don't mean that you should litter your work with adjectives and adverbs. Rather, if you tell the reader that the musician you interviewed preferred to sit behind the piano watching the post-gig party unfold, the reader can guess that he is quite reserved without you having to say it directly. It gives the reader a chance to draw his or her own conclusions and to build a picture in their own mind of what this character is like.

Similarly, describing the character's surroundings can speak volumes about his or her personality. For example, if you are interviewing a Group Chief Executive of a multi-national company and you describe his office as plain and understated with no hint of opulence, then the reader can form a mental image of the person that builds as you progress. You can layer more description on this by paying attention to his mannerisms, the tone of his voice, how his personnel react to him. All these small observational details help to build the picture.

In the same way, describing what you see, hear, smell, taste and touch when you visit various locations can inform your travel writing, spicing up your descriptions and making the destination dance before the eyes of the reader.

Insight – use local idioms

Travel writers will often pick up local nicknames for dishes or attractions
and use these foreign names (plus a brief translation) in their descriptions to
transport the reader to the location and to make it sound suitably exotic and
enticing.

STAY OPEN-MINDED

Sometimes, when you start researching a subject for a creative
non-fiction project, you discover facts that contradict the image you
had formed of that character. Perhaps the great-uncle whose heroic
actions in World War I form the basis of your story was actually
brutal to his wife and children on his return from the battlefields.
Does this change your attitude to him? Will you leave this aspect of
his personality from your readers so that you preserve his unflawed
heroic image?

When you start to investigate more closely into family myths or into
your own assumptions about the past, you have to be prepared for
surprises. And these cannot be swept under the carpet. You must
remain flexible and open-minded, even if your discoveries are
unsettling.

CHARACTERISATION EXERCISES

Exercise one – unfamiliar situation

▶ Take a character from your creative non-fiction project and put him or her into an unfamiliar situation to see how they handle it.
▶ You can choose any situation, possibly even from a different era. For example, s/he is on the way to an important meeting when an accident happens in front of them (pedestrian knocked down by a car/horse). How does s/he react?
▶ Describe the scene. This test of your character's integrity gives you insight into the sort of choices s/he might make. Remember, the characters we relate most easily to are usually flawed in some way.

Exercise two – monologue exercise

▶ Interview an elderly relative or friend about a key period in their life. If you have no surviving elderly relatives, ask a family member to tell you in detail about an episode in the life of a parent or grandparent. It could be an air raid, an elopement, a premature birth, a first job, an overseas trip… it is up to your interviewee.
▶ Now write the scene in the first person voice as if it had happened to you and describe it in the present tense. Write about 250 words and tell the story so that reader feels as if they were at the event and as if they knew you.
▶ If the original interviewee is still around, let them read your account and see how close you came to their experience and emotions.

(Contd.)

Exercise three – perspective exercise

▶ Imagine you are the best man at your own wedding and you have
to write a speech telling the wedding guests something about you
the bride/bridegroom, singing your praises and including a witty
anecdote from your life.

▶ Now, in the interests of seeing a different viewpoint, imagine
the same speech written by an ex-lover or a disgruntled
boss/employee. If you dare, write the speech again from the
perspective of a person who is not your biggest fan.

8

Writing history books

In this chapter you will learn:
- *why history books are so popular*
- *when to use personal narrative*
- *how to find primary and secondary research sources*
- *how to bring historical figures to life.*

Once the preserve of scholars, history books are now one of the best-selling and most popular categories of all non-fiction publishing. In fact, sales of history books in 2009 were at an all time high since records began in 2001, according to the Nielsen report on UK Total Consumer Market Trends. The genre covers every aspect of history, ranging from military history through biographies of historical figures to local history books.

The current popularity of history books is thanks, in large measure, to the success of one book in particular. Published in 1998, *Stalingrad* by Anthony Beevor revolutionized how the public viewed history books and how they were written. The book won the first Samuel Johnson Prize for non-fiction, the Wolfson History Prize and the Hawthornden Prize for Literature in 1999. Yet what is more astonishing for a history book at that time, is that it managed to cross from specialist non-fiction into mainstream books sales, enjoying best-seller success.

The key to *Stalingrad*'s popularity, quite apart from its excellence as an example of historiography, is the fact that it is first and foremost a thumping good read. Beevor obviously bases his writing on solid scholarship and research but it is his narrative of the struggle of the common soldier during the battle for Stalingrad – which he shows in all its chaos and utter horror – that makes the book so compelling and exciting. It could be argued that this is the book that started the current trend for personal narrative in history.

What is personal narrative?

In essence, personal narrative is about writing history 'from the bottom up'. It tells the story of an historical event with the emphasis firmly on how it affected the individuals involved; the true life stories. It gives the reader a chance to understand what it might have been like for those people who were there at that moment in time.

That is not to say that the factual details are not still present. If you choose to write historical non-fiction using this particular style, then you will still have to thoroughly research and know your subject and you must provide the facts wholly and truthfully, but you are able to enliven the story with personal accounts that bring the human element to the fore.

There are those who might argue that this brings non-fiction historical books too close to fiction, but as long as you base your personal accounts on primary sources (see below) and you give them a context in historical fact, then you are simply helping to bring actual past events to life for your reader through the eyes of real characters, albeit that they are not famous.

OTHER STYLES OF HISTORICAL WRITING

If personal narrative is not a style that appeals, do not worry: publishers realize that there are many ways to successfully write history books. If we continue to use the example of *Stalingrad*, two years after its publication, another strong account of the same battle was published to great critical acclaim. *Stalingrad: The Infernal Cauldron* by Stephen Walsh covers much the same ground but it is in a completely different style. It is a military history and his narrative looks at the logistics and tactical planning. It is a military account that discusses not only the battle itself, but also the limits of German national power and the wisdom (or otherwise) of using certain tactics. Both books are excellent accounts of the battle for Stalingrad, but one incorporates personal detail, while the other focuses on military specifics and contexts, and as such these books probably appeal to different audiences. Both found publishers – and that is the point: there are many different ways to approach the same subject.

You simply have to find something original to say in whichever way best suits your personal style.

Whether you choose to write from a personal perspective or to concentrate on factual detail in the 'classic' way, and whether you write on military history, a biography of a past public figure, local history or historical books for children, the success of your project will rest on your ability to communicate your passion for the subject, and on a thorough grounding in the facts.

Primary and secondary source research

Perhaps you are an expert in a particular period of history. More likely you are an enthusiast, in which case, before writing your book you must spend as much time as possible getting to know your subject. I say this because one of the greatest skills of a good history writer is to be able to help newcomers to the subject to understand, engage and enjoy the period or the character as you do.

You can start your research on the internet from the comfort of your home but there is a good chance that you will have to venture further afield to visit specialist libraries, museums, historical societies, corporate archives, newspaper and local record offices and so on, especially if your subject matter is geographically-based elsewhere. For historical books, perhaps more than any other genre of non-fiction writing, the importance of getting primary as well as secondary source research information is paramount.

WHAT IS A PRIMARY SOURCE?

Any document that was created at the time of the event or subject that you are writing about, or by people who observed or were participants in that event or topic can be considered a primary source. It can be in the form of written texts, photographs, paintings, objects; it is not what it is that makes it a primary source but when it was made. For example, if you were writing a book about the Lancashire woollen mills during the late nineteenth century, you could look for primary sources that might include:

▶ Lancashire newspapers circa 1870–1900
▶ photographs taken during that period showing the mills and their workers/owners
▶ associated mill housing records and manuscripts

- census records concerning Lancashire residents for 1871–1901
- maps that show the locations of the mills and the associated housing
- novels of the day that describe the mills, such as Mrs Gaskell's *Mary Barton* (1848)
- music of the day, such as ballads and work songs that were sung or written during the time you are researching
- a loom or skein winder used at the time
- autobiographies of the mill owners of the period, even if published later
- oral histories of mill workers and owners (although not a historian's comments on those oral histories which would be a secondary source).

If you come across a book written by a historian about your chosen topic, this is not a primary source because it is twice removed from the actual event or subject you are writing about. Although it is valuable, you would still want primary source material, if possible, to verify what the historian was saying.

Once you have found your primary sources, you need to ask yourself certain questions so that you can accurately interpret their meaning for your modern-day audience. For example, who is the author and why did he or she create the document – was it private or in the public domain? If the document was published, for which audience was it intended and did that affect the slant of the document? How did it affect its intended audience and how would it be received by those who were not supposed to see it?

Sometimes primary sources trigger a whole train of thought that could perhaps lead your book in a totally unimagined direction. This is why good research is essential before you formulate a rigid idea of what structure your book will take.

WHAT IS A SECONDARY SOURCE?

As you start to gather your research, it can be illuminating to find out what other scholars and historians have written about your subject. These books and papers are known as secondary sources. Some may even have used the same primary sources as you are thinking of using, but they may have drawn different conclusions from those sources than you, or be looking at the subject from a different angle.

You will find as you start to look for books in libraries and those that you come across in the bibliographies of other historians that the same titles will come up again and again. These should be top of your list of reading matter together with the most recently published books (as this gives you an insight into your competition) but keep looking for secondary sources until you think you have exhausted the most important existing secondary literature on your topic. Then you are ready to compile your notes, and to finally get writing.

Compiling your notes

Now you have identified the general themes of your book, found your primary and secondary research material and identified resources for photographs and illustrations (if applicable), you can start to sort the material into categories for different chapters. At this point, it will become clear whether or not you have any areas that are weaker or shorter than others that will need more research. Or perhaps you will have to rethink your chapter outline and incorporate some subjects into other chapters.

Whether you choose to keep handwritten notes on index cards or to electronically file items on your computer, the underlying principle must be that you have an orderly system that allows you to find information easily and that clearly documents sources because you will need this information for your bibliography and for your publisher.

Writing gripping history

A certain amount of planning is required when writing a history book, yet you may well find that the goalposts move as you research your project and as new and interesting facts or accounts come to light. For example, you may have thought that you were writing a straightforward textbook on your subject but, if you uncover some amazing previously unpublished photographs, then you may want to rethink your plan and produce a photographic coffee table book. Other things to consider when planning and writing a history book might include the following.

FINDING THE RIGHT HISTORICAL TOPIC

It is rare that you end up writing a historical book by chance. In most cases, there is a period of history that holds a special fascination for you or you have a connection with a place that means that its local history is of particular interest to you. Once you have identified your interest, you can narrow down the topic to a more focused theme that might be suitable as the basis of a book. For example, you may be interested in the Italian Renaissance period but rather than trying to cover this 400-year epoch in detail, it might be better to focus on one aspect of it – for example, the Borgias' political machinations, Florence under the Medicis or even the birth of modern science.

In part due to the immediacy of modern communication, history is no longer confined to events that happened decades or centuries ago. In military history, for example, people are now writing about the conflict in Iraq and even Afghanistan. So you can throw your net pretty wide when choosing your historical subject.

Apart from knowledge and interest, the only other thing that should guide your choice of book subject is your instinct. Your topic is something that you will instantly recognize or feel is right for you. It must intrigue and inspire you if it is to engage and captivate your reader. So if you have not already got an idea for your book, start reading around the general subject, and some small detail may catch your eye and inspire your topic.

Once you have narrowed down what it is that you want to write about, at that point, you should have a look at what is already on the market on the subject. Even if there are books on the shelves on your topic, it does not necessarily mean you should be put off – as long as you are taking a different approach, there is a healthy interest in history books and the market can bear several titles within the same area.

BRINGING EVENTS AND CHARACTERS TO LIFE

As a non-fiction writer, you cannot allow your imagination to run riot as a fiction writer can. Your story must remain fully grounded in the facts of your subject but you can put the story in human terms. Through your research you can describe what someone might have seen and felt, relying on their journals for guidance. You can use sensory details to make what happens in history relevant today, because essentially we have not changed. What made people sad or fearful 100 years ago still makes us feel that way today. People can relate to the problems that others faced, even if they faced them 400 years ago. It is the story of ordinary people doing extraordinary things that really resonates with readers.

ILLUSTRATING YOUR BOOK

Photographs and illustrations are not essential but they can certainly help breathe life into a story, especially if it is social or local history. Local newspapers, museums, historical societies and private collections are a great source of original photographs and illustrations. If you do source photographs to accompany your text, remember that you are responsible for permissions and copyright fees, which can mount up, so be selective in your choices.

TIMELY PUBLICATION

A publisher is more likely to take an interest in your book if there is an anniversary or important date that coincides with its publication. This 'hook' not only stimulates public interest but also helps the marketing department to publicize your book and the sales department to persuade bookshops to stock copies. For example, 2015 will be the 200th anniversary of the Battle of Waterloo. There will obviously be a plethora of military histories published to coincide with this important anniversary, not to mention biographies of Wellington, but the link can be fairly tenuous – perhaps a local history on Stratfield Saye House (Wellington's family seat) and its environs could interest a publisher if you tie the idea for the book into the upcoming anniversary of Wellington's biggest victory.

If you do decide to use an impending anniversary or date as a marketing incentive in your proposal to a potential publisher, bear in mind that books need a long schedule between commissioning and publication, so give yourself (and the publisher) plenty of time to write, produce and publish the book in time for the anniversary.

MARKETING

If you have written a local history book, your publisher will almost certainly expect you to plan events around the book's release. Why not give the marketing department a helping hand by developing a lecture series on your book which could go down particularly well at local church groups, women's clubs, service men's clubs and local bookstores.

Insight – take off your rose-coloured spectacles

Most historical biographers write about people that they admire, naturally enough. However, that does not mean that you should only show your subject in glowing terms. Don't allow your admiration for your subject to blind you to their faults. To make a character realistic and interesting, you must show them in every aspect – warts and all, if necessary.

HISTORICAL RESEARCH EXERCISE

▶ Choose a local institution or historical figure to research.
▶ Try to find some primary source information on the subject.
▶ Check with local friends and relatives whether they have ever heard that specific fact about the person/institution and also check out some secondary sources to see if your research is corroborated.
▶ If you are sufficiently interested, why not try to write a 3,000-word feature on the subject?

9

Writing personal histories

In this chapter you will learn:
- *how to write a memoir*
- *how to research and write a biography*
- *how to bring family histories to life*.

Writing a personal history is the umbrella term that includes:

▶ memoir writing
▶ biographies and autobiographies
▶ journal and diary writing
▶ letters
▶ family histories.

It is a way of recording and preserving memories and experiences, whether they are your own or someone else's, for posterity. And although once written largely for personal motives and private consumption, certain types of personal writing are becoming highly publishable. Memoirs, autobiographies and biographies – not just of the rich and famous – have been selling in increasing quantities in recent years, partly due to the rise in popularity of the hobby of genealogy (the study of family history) and also due to the spectacular viewing figures for programmes such as *Who Do You Think You Are?* and similar social history programmes.

Is there a member of your family whose story really should be told? Do you want to share the details of a particular important event in your life? Perhaps you come from a long line of adventurers and your family history will capture the imagination of a wider audience. In this chapter, we are going to look at three specific examples of personal writing, namely biography, memoir writing and family history.

Writing a biography

A biography can be about a relative or friend, idol or hero, and that person can be dead or alive. The important thing is that the person is special to you in some way. Once you have identified the subject of your biography, the digging for background information begins. Writing a biography of a family member is one way to preserve the person's life story for future generations of the family. If the subject is still alive, it could possibly strengthen relationships with him or her, or at the very least help your family to understand the individual better. You may want the book to be strictly for family use and hence decide to self-publish or produce an e-book, or you might find that the person's life that you are chronicling is of wider interest, in which case, you could seek a publisher. Of course, your subject could be someone whose exploits you have stumbled across through your work or hobby, and you find sufficiently intriguing to want to write about them. They do not have to be someone you know or to whom you are related.

If you decide to send your manuscript to a publisher or agent, you must be confident that the story is sufficiently compelling and unusual to persuade them to take it on. Be honest with yourself – or if you feel it is impossible to be impartial – describe the contents of your proposed biography to neutral friends/colleagues to find out if they would want to read such a book. If your book is accepted and published, your story will become part of the popular record.

Even if you decide not to publish, writing a biography can be therapeutic. It is a form of self-counselling in a way and often turns up insights into how you feel and relate, and not just to the subject of your book. Writing a biography of a family member can also build bridges when a family is estranged either by distance or dispute.

For the purposes of this chapter, we will concentrate on the necessary steps for writing the biography of a family member but the principles hold true for writing about an inspiring idol.

INTERVIEWING FAMILY AND FRIENDS

If the subject of your biography is still alive, he or she is the first person to speak to, since your job will be so much easier if you have his or her blessing, participation and help for the project.

Technically, it is not essential to have such approval but the task is disproportionately harder if you meet resistance from the subject. Explain why you want to write their story and what you think readers might learn from their life. Don't be surprised if the subject is shocked and uncomprehending as to why you should be interested; this is a common reaction, so do not be deterred.

If the person consents, ask them to make it clear to other members of the family and friends that you have their support. If the subject of your biography is no longer living, then your first port of call is his or her closest living relatives, to seek their support.

Once you have the subject, relatives and friends on your side, you can arrange to interview them individually. Start with your subject, if still alive, and allow plenty of time. In reality, you will probably need several interviews spaced over a number of weeks, especially if the person is elderly. Have a digital tape recorder or camcorder for the interviews, as this makes note taking much easier and guarantees accuracy. Remember to keep and file the tapes for future reference. Questions you might like to ask the person include details about:

▶ his/her childhood, parents and youth
▶ major life events
▶ significant achievements
▶ current goals or aspirations.

Encourage the person to recount stories with as much detail and as vividly as possible, remembering exact names, dates and locations wherever possible.

When you come to interview the subject's relatives, friends and colleagues, do not be afraid to ask them tough questions. Obviously, you want to hear about the subject's strengths and assets, but you should also include material that perhaps does not show the person in the most favourable light. Try to find out as much as possible from each interviewee. You may well find that their account leads to other people who might have information about your relative, or to useful research documents.

RESEARCH DOCUMENTS

Relatives may be able to turn up personal correspondence, diaries, photographs and wills. You can also make use of the local library, newspaper and records offices together with online searches to find court records, probate, newspaper clippings, magazine articles, census, obituaries, church and land records, all of which may yield details of your subject's life.

Looking at the social and cultural history of the time and location can also cast light on your relative's life and set their feats/achievements in the context of his or her specific era and environment.

ORGANIZE YOUR RESEARCH AND THOUGHTS

You will certainly have collected a mass of research information and it helps to take time out to think about how your biography will come together long before you consider writing. For example, have you discovered any information that makes you reassess the person and how you portray them? What makes this person special and interesting (not just to you but to a reader)? What were the milestone events of his or her life? Has he or she been an influence on family, society or a profession? In essence, you need to give thought to which aspects of the person's life you want to highlight.

At this stage, you can create a chapter outline and categorize your research into the relevant chapters. As you start to pull each chapter together, you can re-contact the subject of your biography or other interviewees to fill in any missing information or to clarify facts.

When writing, you do not need to start at birth and go through the life and events chronologically. In fact, that can be most dull. Instead, focus on periods, activities and events that are of interest and could form a chapter. Then break down each chapter into further sections, making notes as you go to remind you where certain anecdotes and stories fit in.

Insight – use social networking sites

Social networking sites such as Facebook and MySpace can be useful when you're life writing as they are a good way to help you to find school friends, old acquaintances and relations that you have lost touch with.

WRITING YOUR BIOGRAPHY

If you want to bring your character to life, you need to describe the small details such as his or her appearance, habits, mannerisms, and way of speaking/walking and how you/they felt – whatever marks him or her out as an individual – as well as their more significant actions and achievements. Try to avoid obvious or overused descriptions such as 'slim' or 'good looking', rather choose something more telling and specific to the individual. If you can describe the person's surroundings and environment, it helps the reader to form a mental image and to place the person and their actions in a social context.

Make sure you introduce and describe other players in the story. In this way, the reader can find those they like and those they dislike, and then they begin to care about what happens to them. Be wary of going into too much detail, or using too many adjectives and adverbs in your descriptive writing. When you edit your work, you can remove many of these words and you will be surprised at how much tighter the writing becomes.

Once completed, you can show your manuscript to the person you have written about and ask for their feedback and to point out any inaccuracies. The person may not like everything you have written but that does not mean you have to edit those sections. This is your book and you are simply asking for feedback as a matter of courtesy. Nonetheless, you have to weigh up whether it is worth publishing a biography that might upset its subject or cause harm to your relationship with that relative or the wider family. If you are not aiming for a 'tell all' exposé, then you might want to take their comments into account and tone down any sections that are private or which might be inappropriate. You could also show your manuscript to family members and friends for feedback and criticism, again with the proviso that you may or may not take the comments on board and make changes.

Bear in mind that if you defame a person's character in print, you are opening yourself up to a libel action. The truth can be told in print but you must make every effort to disguise the identity of individuals mentioned if you or your publisher believes that what you are saying is likely to be considered libellous. In any event, you may wish to change names to protect identities, in which case, you simply put a disclaimer at the front of your book stating that some names and identifying details have been changed – this is common practice.

GETTING YOUR BIOGRAPHY PUBLISHED

There was a time when the only biographies that sold were those of celebrities or famous historical figures, but there has been a growing interest in popular history so the biographies of ordinary men and women can now be found on the shelves. Nonetheless, I would be raising your hopes unfairly if I failed to point out that this is an extremely competitive sector of the publishing market and your biography will have to be exceptionally well written and tell an unusual and gripping tale to stand any chance of being accepted.

For most biography writers, the next option is self-publishing or e-publishing. You are unlikely to make your fortune using this route, but you can sell books into specialist markets or to local outlets, where there is a connection to the subject. If the biography means you become an expert on a specific event or period, you might find that you are called upon occasionally as a speaker.

Autobiographies

If you think your own life story is interesting and worth telling, then why not write your autobiography? The same research rules apply as for writing a biography but obviously, since you are the main subject, you record or write your own recollections of key events and periods of your life. Although in some ways it is easier to write an autobiography because you should meet with no resistance and information is on tap, in another way, it becomes harder. This is because it is difficult to be impartial or to judge what is of interest to your reader when it is your own story. It is probably worth writing a draft manuscript and then showing it to supportive but sufficiently critical friends or relatives for candid feedback.

Insight – deal with self-consciousness

Almost all of the students on my writing courses initially find it hard to read their personal writing to an audience. If you're self-conscious about your work, then writing an online blog is a digital form of life-writing that can be a valuable way to become comfortable with revealing yourself and your personal experiences. If you're a technophobe, why not read some excerpts from your writing to a selected group of friends instead.

Writing a memoir

There is often confusion among writers about what is a memoir and what is an autobiography. Basically, the major difference is that an autobiography can span a long period of time, while a memoir tends to focus on events related to a specific theme. For example, Frank McCourt's *Angela's Ashes* is about coming of age, a very popular topic for memoirs, while *Purge: Rehab Diaries* by Nicole Johns covers the other big memoir topic of eating disorders. However, the topic can be anything ranging from an abusive spouse to dealing with a major illness or even your relationship with your pet; witness *Marley and Me* by John Grogan.

The other way in which a memoir might differ from an autobiography is that although both are non-fiction, a memoir often reads more like a novel, calling on creative non-fiction techniques to bring events to life, which can make the story more compelling for the reader, even if the author is not a celebrity. For this reason, memoirs can be more popular than autobiographies.

If you decide you would like to write your own memoir, be prepared for an emotional and complex journey of self-discovery and soul-searching. Questioning yourself on how much of what you are writing is the truth and what is your memory playing tricks on you, or reliving traumatic or difficult personal territory can be emotionally exhausting. It will demand emotional honesty, authenticity and courage. However, memoir writing can also be a therapeutic and beneficial experience that can be highly rewarding, whether or not you hope to publish the end product. Any form of personal writing is a way of breaking down the barriers between self and others. As you reveal yourself, it can be an uncomfortable experience, especially at first. If this feeling persists, you could consider joining a memoir writing group or post personal stories online to get comfortable with revealing yourself and your private thoughts.

GETTING STARTED

Memoir writing is not simply about sitting down and letting your story spill out onto the page. For your memoir to be readable and accessible to others, it requires a certain amount of planning and preparation. Firstly you need to consider what you are going to write about – remember a memoir considers one aspect or theme or a particular period of your life. Once you have decided on your topic, then it helps you to focus when researching and writing. This should help you to decide what is relevant, what is unnecessary, and hopefully, this approach will keep you on track.

Although memoirs can be told chronologically, in a similar fashion to autobiography, you also have the freedom to play around with the order of events. Perhaps you might like to use recollection to heighten the impact of your story. As long as you keep your theme in mind and keep the content relevant, you can move backwards and forwards in time, but bear in mind that too much jumping around might confuse your reader.

RESEARCH

You might think that because this is your own story, that research will not be necessary. However, our memories are notoriously inaccurate, as our brains tend to recall the main aspect of events but forget some of the details. Sometimes research can help you to remember things that you have forgotten or to clarify things that are unclear. Perhaps looking at old photographs and films from the time, or reading old journals and newspapers, even smelling familiar scents could help you to recall how you felt at the time or even to relive some of the experiences. If you can incorporate these feelings into your memoir, it will enhance the story for the reader.

You do not have to rely solely on your own memory of events. You can ask other people who were involved for their recollections, which may or may not corroborate your version of events. Gaining the perspective of others can provide additional detail and insight that will enhance and embellish your story. Hearing others' recollections of an event that you have also experienced can sometimes trigger lost memories for you.

If you plan to include references to popular culture or historical/ cultural events, make sure you check your facts for accuracy. Getting dates and details wrong can harm your credibility with your reader. Since a memoir is a true story, if you include factual errors, it can cast doubt on other aspects of your story. So check and recheck the facts, even those of your personal history (which you might think are indisputable) as the accuracy of this information is crucial to the credibility of your main story.

MEMOIR WRITING TIPS

Once you start to write the following pointers may prove helpful.

Keep it personal It is perfectly acceptable, even desirable to write a memoir in the first person, as this is your personal interpretation of events and this is your memoir.

Bring your story to life There is more to memoir writing than just capturing an aspect of your personal history. It needs to be a story; a good read. Although it is a real event, you can still be creative and make your story gripping.

Stay focused Even if a scene or event that you recount is action-packed and thrilling, ask yourself 'Is it relevant to my theme?' Do not be tempted to include action for the sake of it because too many cul-de-sacs will simply frustrate your reader.

Avoid excluding your reader Bear in mind that your reader was not present at the events that you describe, so using 'insider jokes' will make them feel excluded. If you must make such references, make sure you give some background to explain the context so the reader understands and feels part of it.

Use dialogue Capturing what people say in a given situation is a great way to reveal their character. You do not have to relay a verbatim account of the conversation, as long as the dialogue captures the essence of what was said. Check to make sure that the people involved are satisfied that your words are a true reflection of what was said or meant. Reading about what people actually said to each other gives an authenticity to your story, and dialogue can be particularly powerful when recounted in emotionally charged situations such as a humorous or sad occasion.

Be sensitive to those you portray This does not mean that you have to show everyone in a good light. Rather, if you are going to include text that could be considered controversial, you may wish to disguise the identity of the individual.

The devil is in the detail What may seem an insignificant detail may be the one thing that your reader completely recognizes. It is the detail that brings that reader into your world, as you share what you saw and what you felt. Of course, this means that you are probably revealing personal and intimate thoughts and secrets, which is not necessarily easy, but through these disclosures, your reader gains a far deeper and more insightful understanding of events.

Be patient A good memoir does not appear overnight. Often you become overly critical of your early efforts, believing it is of no interest, not good enough, too boring or too similar to others, but you need to persevere. Move past those concerns and as you revisit the material with fresh eyes, often the real story emerges. Stick with it and you will be rewarded.

Writing a family history

Does your family harbour a secret? Are you sitting on a stash of grandma's love letters, returned to her when her fiancé was killed at Ypres in World War I? What about that box of family photos and memorabilia that is sitting in the loft? All of these scenarios and more are the reason why countless people decide to write a family history. In addition, as genealogy becomes increasingly popular as a hobby, so more and more people are considering joining the throng of those writing their family history.

However, if you are a would-be writer approaching this project as a potential publishing venture, rather than an individual who simply wants to record family details for future generations, then is a family history a good publishing vehicle? In truth, the answer is probably 'No' if you are considering finding a traditional publisher to produce your book. Unless your family has famous or notable ancestors, or if you have some exceptional thread that runs through the generations, then a publisher is unlikely to take you on. For example, Richard Moore's *Leeches to Lasers* follows eight generations of medical practitioners, effectively telling the family history as well as describing the history of medicine since the 1740s. A publisher could see how this family history book would have a wider appeal. If your family is interesting to its members but unremarkable in any other way, then you are unlikely to tempt a publisher.

Nevertheless, you could still write your family history with publication in mind. You could think of it as a self-publishing venture or an e-book. This way, it is in a format that will preserve your lineage for posterity and you still get the experience of planning, researching and writing a book, and seeing it in print.

PLANNING YOUR FAMILY HISTORY

A family history can encompass a wide time span and vast numbers of individuals, which is a fairly daunting prospect. So you would be well advised to give thought to what you want to achieve and how you want to achieve it from the outset.

Choose a structure Your book does not have to be a straightforward list of characters and events since great-great-great grandfather Josiah. You can make your book a more interesting prospect for the reader if you write it as a narrative that focuses on specific events or episodes in the life of selected ancestors. Or why not have a theme, such as family recipes that have been handed down, as a hook to describe the cook and his/her family and their exploits. Perhaps you are lucky enough to have a large number of family photographs, in which case you could produce a photo book and combine it with family trees and personal stories to bring those photos to life.

Choose your characters You might decide that you are going to focus on a single line of descent, starting with the earliest known ancestor with a specific surname, until you reach yourself. Or if your ancestors emigrated, then you might choose to start with the émigré couple and follow all their descendants in their new homeland.

As a good yardstick for readability, why not choose the characters that grabbed your interest. There is a good chance that they are the most spirited individuals, and if they intrigue you and live in your mind, there is every chance they will come alive for your reader too. Whatever your criteria for choosing the players in your story, what you want to avoid is a dry list of births, marriages and deaths, which leads to chronological boredom. If you choose the right characters and tell their story, you will create an intriguing story.

Choose a theme Is there a common idea or theme that threads its way through the generations? Rather than telling individual stories, it is useful to identify a general theme for your story. Were your ancestors a rebellious bunch? Or were they explorers, visionaries or inventors? Is there a trade or profession that features largely down the years? Does immigration/migration loom large in your history? Is yours a rags-to-riches story? Choosing a plot helps to give your family history a focus.

Choose a starting point In the same way that you cherry-pick your most interesting characters, so you can choose an interesting part of their story from whence to start your narrative. In this way, you can grab your reader's attention from the outset with an exciting, happy or tragic event or conflict.

THOROUGH RESEARCH

It is important to make your reader feel like they are witnessing your ancestors' lives unfolding. For their stories to be credible, you must have good background research not only on their lives but also on the social history of that era. To get a feel for this, you need to read town and city histories about that specific period. Timelines of wars, natural disasters, epidemics and economic climates can put your ancestor's story into broader context. More general reading on fashions, food, art and lifestyles of the time can all be informative. If you come across maps, photos and other illustrations, these make great support material too.

Closer to home, any first-hand accounts written by your ancestors – diary entries, journals, letters, military accounts, obituaries – are well worth including, plus any interesting contemporary accounts that mention your ancestor such as newspaper cuttings, records from neighbours and other family members. You can take brief excerpts that support your story and include a source citation to the original record.

Why not interview your living relatives, not only to corroborate family myths but also to use their personal accounts in your story? If you have a large family, you may want to email or send out a questionnaire aimed at saving the individual's time and hopefully helping to maintain their support.

Similarly, you could write down the bare bones of your research thus far plus vital statistics (such as names, births, marriages and deaths) on a worksheet which you send out to relatives, asking them to fill in any gaps with additional information and anecdotes. You can also put out the request for photographs at the same time.

Once you get back the questionnaires and worksheets, and you have collected all your research together, you can produce a timeline for each of the ancestors that you plan to feature in your history. From this, you can form a chapter outline and also identify any gaps in your research that require further investigation. With your research complete, you can order your material to fit in with your chosen theme.

WRITING YOUR FAMILY HISTORY

All good stories have a beginning, middle and an end, and a family history is no different. To make your story as compelling as possible, it needs to be a narrative that people want to read. It can still be a factual account that is fully researched and documented, but by employing some of the following techniques, you can turn dry facts into a captivating family saga.

Getting started Rather than starting your history with the subject's birth, along the lines of 'Joseph Maxwell was born on 18 February 1863 on a farm near Bishops Lydeard in Somerset', why not open your narrative with an interesting event or intriguing aspect of your subject's life? This is far more likely to reel the reader in and maintain their interest.

Make it personal Readers relate to everyday details so include anecdotes, favourite family stories, embarrassing moments, either using their own personal accounts, or telling the story as if they had, using what you have learnt about them through your research.

Style To enliven what can be a dull list of facts, you are aiming to craft your data into a compelling non-fiction narrative, and the best way to do so is to employ fiction writing techniques to tell your story.

Maintain the pace You can keep your story from losing momentum in the middle by keeping your eye on the pace. If you feel it is beginning to slacken, try to rebuild the suspense by including a mystery or leaving something unfinished so that your reader has to move to the next chapter to find out how the tale unfolds.

You can also avoid chronological boredom by adding insights about a character from a different generation. For example, while telling the story of your great-grandfather who left his family in the North-east of England to go gold prospecting in Australia, you could add some boxed copy which is a first-hand account from your grandfather of his childhood memories of his father. It simply gives another twist in the tale and helps to create a rounded picture of the character.

Finish on a high You certainly do not want your family history to trail off into a weak ending. So save something interesting until last. It does not have to be contrived, but nor does it have to end when everyone in the story has died. Chronologically, that may be the end but you can choose to end the story wherever you like; perhaps at the moment of one of the subject's greatest achievements. It is also a temptation for inexperienced writers to try to tie up all lose ends so that everyone lives happily ever after. In reality, life does not always work out that way so do not feel you have to give your family history a happy ending. Rather, choose an episode or situation with impact that will leave a lasting impression, happy or otherwise.

Include appendices When writing a family history in a narrative form, it is not always convenient or possible to work all the facts into the story. In this case, it is useful to add a reference section at the back of the book that is full of genealogical detail, factual summaries, and source citations.

Read and revise Once you have read and revised your first draft, leave it for a few days, if not weeks, and then return to it with fresh eyes. You may then wish to make more revisions. Once you are happy with it, arrange for someone who knows little about your family or the theme to read it and give feedback. You can also ask someone who is knowledgeable about the period or the theme to read it to check facts and for accuracy.

Insight – include a range of accounts

Sometimes it can be interesting if you include varying accounts of the same event in your family history. For example, if you ask five members to recount the story, invariably the accounts differ and some even conflict. This is what makes family history so compelling.

Finding a publisher

Most family histories are self-published and distributed among the wider family. Nonetheless, having completed your story, if you believe it merits publication, you must think of the angle that will most interest a prospective publisher and persuade him or her that there is a market for your book. Ask yourself who might be interested in reading your book. Is it aimed at a general reader or a specialist? Does it touch on cultural issues? Does it offer a new insight into the periods covered or the lifestyles of the personalities included? Could the theme of the book be of interest to hobbyist groups or to tourists visiting the area of its setting?

Make sure your book fits the publishing norm. So it should be somewhere in the region of 25,000 to 40,000 words in length and use a standard print size. You can let a publisher know that photographs and illustrations are available, and send a sample few, but production costs for a photographic book are high, so a publisher may decide against using all your material.

Finally, choose an intriguing title that will catch the eye and pique curiosity. If a manuscript comes across the desk entitled *The Smith Family History* it is scarcely likely to excite. On the other hand, *Potatoes, Pastors and The Pox* might take someone's fancy.

CHARACTER STUDY EXERCISE

▶ Choose a member of your family (s/he can be living or an ancestor) but make sure they are still in living memory.
▶ Interview relatives about this person and get a mental image of what sort of person they are/were.
▶ Write a 750–1,000 word character study that incorporates a story from their personal history.
▶ Allow those relatives to read the character study and to give feedback on its accuracy.

10

New media

In this chapter you will learn:
- *how to write a blog*
- *how to publish an e-book*
- *how to self-publish.*

There has been a media revolution in recent years and there are now an overwhelming number of choices for how and when we consume media. Most importantly for the non-fiction writer, these new developments also allow you to create your own media. Newspapers, magazines and books are no longer the only routes to publication for the non-fiction writer. Developments in IT and printing technology mean that via the new media, which includes blogging, e-books and self-publishing, writers are now able to reach a global audience relatively inexpensively and with ease.

Blogging

It is said that a new blog is launched every second. A blog (a blend of the words 'web' and 'log') is effectively an online diary. However, it is not the sole preserve of those who wish to share their idle musings. Blogs can be a launch pad for the professional writer.

In fact, Julie Powell, the author of *Julie & Julia: 365 Days, 524 Recipes and 1 Tiny Apartment Kitchen*, started out by writing a blog. The 32-year-old New Yorker started the blog, which was basically a series of her reflections on cooking, life and love, when she decided to document her attempts to cook all 524 recipes in Julia Child's 1961 recipe book *Mastering the Art of French Cooking*. As the blog grew in popularity, so a book deal with Penguin followed, eventually spawning the Hollywood film, *Julie & Julia*, starring Meryl Streep. The book has sold more than 100,000 copies worldwide and Powell is now a successful, full-time writer.

Books that are spawned by blogs have created a new word, namely Blooks. There is even a Blooker Prize and Powell's book won the first Lulu Blooker Prize back in 2006. Although some traditional publishers are starting to question whether blog popularity equates to sales, blog to book conversions via traditional publishing houses still happen, although the focus for scouting publishers has shifted from blog popularity to content quality. In 2006, more than 100 bloggers landed book deals in the US and since the trend looks set to continue, a blog could be a useful way for you to practise your writing skills, and who knows, it may even get picked up by an agent or publisher.

SETTING UP A BLOG

For those who are unable to write code for websites (that's probably most of us), there are sites that offer free blogging. The sites are quick and easy to use and you are given your own address to give to friends and clients who may want to take a look. The more popular sites are listed in Taking it further. Once you have chosen your host site, you simply enter your details where it says 'create account'. You move on to the pages where you enter your data, and/or upload any pictures or videos. Then you are set to write your blog. When you are happy with what you have written, you hit 'publish' and your words are live for all to see.

WRITING A BLOG

If anyone is going to read your blog, it is important that it has some real content. So what you have to say should be entertaining and/or informative. It should conform to people's expectations of a good website rather than a good book, which effectively means keeping your sentences short and punchy. This is your platform and, as such, it can reflect your personality, views and opinions. There is no sitting on the fence with a blog. Having said that, you don't want to be too authoritative either.

Blogs can be any length you like but it is hard to read large chunks of text on a computer screen so break your prose into shorter paragraphs, and if necessary, deliver your message in several instalments, for example, 'Grooming your Newfoundland Dog Part I' and 'Grooming your Newfoundland Dog Part II'.

> ## Insight – beware copyright pitfalls
>
> If you are using images, videos or music on your blog, be wary of copyright infringement. Unless you know who has ownership and/or you have permission, you are probably best advised to only use material that you own.

Copyright still applies to blogs so if you quote magazines or books and so on, the permission procedure still applies. Whenever you quote, make sure you credit the source.

BEING SEEN

Although writing a blog is good writing practice, the whole point of a blog is to get your message out to a wide audience. To this end, make sure you mention your subject as often as possible in your first paragraph without labouring the point, as this will help to get your blog prominently listed with the search engines. You can also fill in the section for 'tags'. These are words that you would associate with your blog, which are designed to help it come up in online searches.

If you keep your blog regularly updated with lively, well-written ideas, word will soon spread as friends tell more people. Most blogs are interactive so readers can leave feedback and comments. This is a useful way to source ideas and direction, and to generate further interest from the public.

E-books

The internet has revolutionized the way that book lovers read books. Although many readers believe that they still want the sensual feel of a real 'paper and ink' book, there are many who love the ease of buying e-books online and the fact that they can store thousands of titles on one device. As a reflection of this growing acceptance, the UK sales of e-books rose threefold in 2009. In addition, following the launch of the Amazon Kindle and e-bookstore in the UK in August 2010, the Publishers Association is hopeful that the British market will close the gap with the US market, where e-books made up 15 per cent of overall sales in 2009.

WHAT IS AN E-BOOK?

An e-book is a downloadable data file that can be downloaded and read either on an electronic device known as an electronic reader, or on the computer screen. Palm pilots and readers such as Amazon's Kindle and the Apple iPad (and devices from other manufacturers including Sony and Cool-ER) allow people the potential to store hundreds of books at one time. While not as popular, e-books can also be bought in disc or DVD format to be read via a computer. Not only do e-book publishers sell downloadable books, they are also able to sell a single e-book chapter, at a suitably reduced price.

WHAT'S IN IT FOR AUTHORS?

Well, the good news is that, with the advent of electronic books, comes greater publishing opportunities for authors. Although currently most e-books are fiction, e-publishers distribute all types of books, and there are plenty of openings for the non-fiction writer. And it is not just the novice writer who is choosing e-books – established author Stephen King is publishing a serialized novel solely on the web, and all the early indications are that it will be successful.

Just as in traditional publishing, there are various routes to choose from when publishing an e-book. If you are technologically minded, you can publish your own e-book on your own website or by using e-book publishing software. You can write your book using a standard word processing programme such as Microsoft Word but save it as a PDF file. Once bought, your reader will need a programme such as Adobe Acrobat Reader to read your book. This software is a free programme that is available for download from the Adobe website.

You can charge for your book by accepting credit card payments (for which you need to set up a merchant account with your bank) or through a third-party merchant – such as PayPal – who takes a small transaction fee. These payment options are relatively easy to install on your website and there is plenty of online advice on how to go about it. The beauty of publishing your own e-book is that you set the price and virtually all profits go to you.

Alternatively, you can approach an e-book publisher, and there are many to choose from. For example, with an e-publisher such as e-junkie.com, you pay about $5 (that's £3.15) per month, for unlimited download bandwidth for e-books, though they have a 50 MB storage limit for the account. If you use a company such as PayPal to process the money and credit card orders for your sales, you will end up earning about 90 per cent of the cover price on your e-books, compared to roughly 10–15 per cent if you go through a traditional print publisher. From this point of view, e-publishing makes perfect sense but you are not going to sell any e-books if people cannot find your website.

MARKETING

Most importantly, you need some sort of specialist information to make your e-book desirable, and a way to market it. If you run pilates classes and workshops, for example, then you may well have a wide database of clients who would be delighted to buy your e-book. And you can plug it at every class, workshop and retreat that you run. Alternatively, you could select an e-publisher who will take on the responsibility of distributing your e-book.

However, if you have no client base and no other way of marketing your book to a wider public audience, then the e-book route to publication may not be such a viable option for you after all. Nonetheless, with e-book technology and e-publishing developments changing every day, it is important that you familiarize yourself with this emerging and growing technology as practices will undoubtedly evolve and change. At the very least, you should understand what e-publishing is.

A WORD OF WARNING

At the current time, one of the problems of e-book publishing is piracy. Once downloaded, it is easy for readers to share their e-books with others without paying for them, so robbing you of income. This could either be by emailing the book to friends or by getting a refund for a book but still continuing to use it electronically.

> **Insight – is e-book piracy a threat?**
> I don't doubt that e-book piracy and copyright infringement exist but I am not entirely convinced that it is a serious threat to the majority of e-writers' incomes from e-books. It would certainly have to be proven to be on a large scale before such a threat would deter me from considering e-book publishing as a viable option.

There are preventative measures you can take. For example, you could put a PDF password protection system in place, use an IP tracking system that warns you when multiple users are attempting to use one IP address, or put a time limit on the download period but, for the determined fraudster, there are always ways around these precautions.

Self-publishing

Although in the past some famous authors have self-published, most notably Rudyard Kipling, Mark Twain, Beatrix Potter, Virginia Woolf, and more recently, Booker Prize nominee, Jill Paton Walsh, self-publishing always had a rather tawdry, desperate image. However, in recent years, self-publishing has become a far more popular and acceptable option, largely because authors are less afraid of 'going it alone' but also because it is now seen as a route to attracting a subsequent print publishing deal. Nonetheless, if you self-publish, it is no guarantee that your book is going to sell successfully, or that it will be picked up by a publisher.

The good news for you, since you are reading this book, is that specialist non-fiction is the easiest and most successful form of writing to market effectively after self-publishing, as you know the profile of your readership and perhaps have ways to reach them, namely specialist clubs or journals, subject-specific websites and lectures/workshops and so on. The following suggestions are a collection of reasons that might help you to decide to go down the self-publication route.

10 GOOD REASONS TO SELF-PUBLISH

1 You want to maintain control of how your book looks and reads. Most publishers do not give you, as author, the final approval on copy-editing. With self-publishing, you are in control.
2 If you know that you only want a limited number of copies of a bound book to distribute among family and friends (perhaps a book on your family history, for example), then self-publishing fits the bill.
3 You have a large circulation list, either because you run classes/ courses, you have specialist knowledge and access to the associated specialist network (for example, you are secretary of

the Trabant owners club, or perhaps you have a small specialist business). In this way you can potentially sell a lot of books because you have good marketing outlets.

4 Your book is time-sensitive and you need to get it to the market as soon as possible, so you cannot wait for a traditional publisher to make a decision and to go to print, which can take as long as a year to 18 months.

5 You have had countless rejections from publishers who have all made it clear that, due to its subject matter, it is not going to be a viable book for them. So, if you are publishing a niche market book such as a specialist interest or local history book that will not appeal to a mainstream publisher, self-publishing may be your best and only option.

6 With your book in print, you have a book proposal that is hard to ignore if you want to be noticed by a bigger publisher. That said, a badly written book is as likely to be rejected as a badly written manuscript, so make sure it is a worthwhile project before going down the self-publishing route.

7 If you have sales figures from a self-published book to show to a potential publisher, you have a proven track record which shows there is a market and that is very persuasive.

8 For self-gratification. If money is no object and you simply want to see your book in print, it is ideal.

9 Self-publishing can give your confidence and self-esteem a huge boost. Having your own book in your hands and successfully navigating the self-publishing process is something to be proud of.

10 The saying is 'Success is the best revenge'. So proving to all those mainstream publishers who turned you down that there is a healthy paying audience for your book could be the sweetest success of all.

If you fit into one of the above categories, then self-publishing could be an option for you. Nonetheless, self-publishing is an expensive business and there are drawbacks, so it is not for the faint-hearted or for everyone.

SIX REASONS TO AVOID SELF-PUBLISHING

1 Self-publishing is a costly business and you could lose every penny that you invest in the venture. So, if you are going into self-publishing purely as a means of making money, you may be disappointed. Of course, if the book sells, you stand to make

considerably more money than if you were published via the traditional route because you earn the publisher's share of the profits as well. However, if you end up with a lot of unsold books, these eat in to any potential profit.

Effectively, you bear all the costs up front, as you do not have an advance from a publisher. These costs soon mount up and could include the services of a designer for the jacket cover and layout, editing, proofreading and the largest cost of all, printing. You are unlikely to get the best job by using your local printer, and would be better advised to approach a specialist book printer. Their prices are on a sliding scale – the larger the print run, the lower the cost per book. Although it seems attractive to print 2,000 books at a price of £3,000 rather than 1,000 books at £2,500, you must be brutally honest with yourself about how many books you can realistically sell. If you are left with 1,200 of the 2,000 books, then in real terms, the price per book has risen substantially – and you are left storing 800 unwanted books.

2 One of the greatest benefits of having a publisher is being able to draw on their accumulated expertise. Without their professional advice and another pair of fresh eyes, you can make fundamental errors.

3 You will have to devote a considerable amount of time to your self-publishing venture. If you are working full-time, can you invest enough time in finding and dealing with editors, proof-readers, typesetters and printers?

4 If your budget will not stretch to hiring professional help, you will have to cover these roles yourself. Are you proficient enough to edit, proofread and design your own book?

5 If your ambition is to be able to walk into any high street bookstore and see your book on the shelf, you are unlikely to realize your dream if you self-publish. Marketing your book and getting it into bookstores is probably the hardest part of any self-publishing venture. Most booksellers will expect a heavy discount, and some of the bigger chains only buy on a national basis, leaving the manager of your local store with his hands tied. Some bookstores do not deal with small independent publishers, let alone an individual with a single self-published book. If you do get some interest from a shop, you will have to obtain an ISBN (International Standard Book Number) and barcode for

your book, again at additional cost. Unless you can market your book directly to your buying readership, for example, via your own or a specialist website, via a mailing list or through talks/classes and so on, getting copies into the shops can be an uphill struggle.

6 Finally, there is no guarantee that having a final product will convince a publisher to take a chance on you. Although some might be persuaded by your dedication and determination, others could be put off by the fact that the book is now the finished article, and they have little scope for input.

GOING IT ALONE

If you are going to go completely down the do-it-yourself route to publication, then you will be well advised to do your homework before you start. Research the subject fully using the internet or dedicated self-publishing books (see Taking it further) and make sure you get a selection of quotes from suppliers for each stage of the process since charges vary considerably. If you are prepared to learn on the job by asking plenty of questions, then this can be an extremely fulfilling experience, albeit time consuming.

SELF-PUBLISHING SERVICES

If going it alone is too daunting, there are companies who specialize in offering self-publishing packages to the would-be writer. You can select which services you require or you can go for the complete package. Not only does this take some of the headache and time-drain out of self-publishing, but it also leaves you in control. Effectively, you are buying selected services but you remain the publisher. Once again, it is worth shopping around for the most competitively priced services since fees can vary substantially, and make sure you know what you are getting in return for you money.

You are probably looking at an initial print run of between 500 and 1,000 copies of your book. Unfortunately, the printing and binding of such a modest number of copies is likely to make the service fairly expensive, as printing and binding are far and away the most expensive part of the process.

VANITY PUBLISHING

You should not confuse self-publishing with vanity publishing, which is a far more sinister proposition. The vanity press, who variously describe their services as 'subsidy publishing', 'joint venture publishing' or even 'co-contributing publishing partners' will seek out your business by advertising their services in the classified ads of national newspapers and magazines. Vanity publishers exploit the naïve and the desperate. They will give you glowing feedback on the quality of your writing and unrealistically high predictions on potential sales figures. They will always ask you for money (or a 'contribution' as some quaintly put it) – which can easily stretch to anything from £2,000 to £10,000 – but you rarely receive what you are expecting. For example, you may pay over the odds for getting your book printed but the vanity publisher will have failed to mention that this price does not include binding, so your books turn up as loose-leaf manuscripts.

Once you have paid them to publish your book, there is no incentive for them to do any more. So promises that they will sell the book to bookstores and so on are rarely – if ever – met. In all probability, all the marketing will be left to you. And even if these vanity publishers were to approach a reviewer or bookshop, most are wise to these companies. Most bookshops do not stock their products, reasoning that the majority of books that end up on the vanity press lists are those that have been rejected by conventional publishers (even if this does not apply to your book). So, how do you spot a vanity publisher as opposed to a *bona fide* self-publishing service? Here are a few tips:

▶ Beware advertisements saying 'Authors wanted!' Most conventional publishers and self-publishing houses are inundated with manuscripts and do not need to advertise.
▶ Undertakings to print 'up to 1,000 copies' or to send press releases to 'up to 25 reviewers' should be viewed with scepticism.
▶ Be suspicious of flattery and outrageous claims for sales figures. Most *bona fide* publishers are cautious about handing out praise or over-egging expectations.

- ▶ The offer of a large royalty figure – sometimes up to 30 per cent – should ring alarm bells. The industry standard is around 10 per cent.
- ▶ Be cautious of 'free copy' offers. You have already covered production costs, but after you receive your 'ten free copies' you are likely to be offered more copies only if you make a further payment.
- ▶ If they are unable to furnish your book with an ISBN (International Standard Book Number), which allows a book to be sold by retailers, they are a vanity publisher.
- ▶ A self-publishing company will allow you to have your own 'publishing house' name on the book rather than their own.
- ▶ Ask to speak to other clients who have had their books published through their services. If they are genuine, there should be no reason why they cannot put you in touch, with that person's consent, of course.
- ▶ If they give you a list of books that they have published, check them out on an internet bookstore. If these appear and are listed under different 'publisher' names, then they are authentic self-publishers.
- ▶ Ask to see a copy of a book that they have published. Production values tend to be poor with vanity publishers.

Print-on-demand

As the name suggests, print-on-demand (POD) or available-on-demand (AOD) publishing means you can order as many or as few copies of your book as you want because it is digitally printed rather than produced on a printing press, as in conventional printing. Once again, the problem with this route to publication is after-sales service. A POD publisher is not going to market your book and the only way you can reach potential readers is through your own marketing and sales efforts (e.g. through your website). Nonetheless, many mainstream publishers now have POD services as this can be a very attractive option for books that only sell a handful of copies each year but that the publisher wants to keep on their list.

As with all other forms of self-publishing, it pays to shop around. Make sure your POD service gives a firm guarantee about the final price to you (not cheap, I'll wager), the retail price and delivery dates. I recommend that you get the publishing contract checked out by the Society of Authors or a lawyer specializing in publishing contracts, as there can be clauses within it that may tie you in to giving your POD publisher a share of future earnings.

Print-on-demand publishing can be a useful option for authors who have a previously published book that has been out of print for some years that they would like to resurrect in small numbers. If you find yourself in this situation, you must make sure in writing that all rights have reverted to you from the original publisher and layout may have to be changed, as copyright in 'the typographical arrangement of the published edition' which is vested in the publisher lasts 25 years from first publication.

BLOG-WRITING EXERCISE

▶ Set yourself the challenge of writing a daily or weekly blog.
▶ Investigate the options and set up an account and then get
  blogging.
▶ Tell your friends and family about it and get them to leave
  feedback – it could be revealing and will certainly give you some
  insight into whether or not you have enough material on your
  intended subject.
▶ If you do not want to spend money on this exercise, you can
  always write a daily blog in a journal format, which you review
  at the end of a set period.

11

Travel writing

In this chapter you will learn:
- *how to make the familiar sound exciting*
- *the importance of paying attention to your surroundings*
- *how to put yourself in the picture*
- *how to inform and evoke in equal measure.*

Travel writing is undoubtedly one of the hardest sectors of the market to break into, not only because there are hundreds of specialist travel writers on hand, but also because it has occurred to most freelance journalists to make some extra cash by writing a feature about their holidays on their return and trying to sell it. Nonetheless, there are a lot of outlets for travel writing – there are specialist magazines and most general consumer magazines and newspapers also have a travel section. And since going on overseas press trips is time consuming, specialist travel writers cannot fill all the slots.

So, if you love to sit and watch the world go by, travel writing could be the genre for you. It is a prerequisite of good travelogue that you take time to simply observe what is going on around you and to look for the small details that make a place unique. As a travel writer, your job is to help the reader to grasp the unfamiliar, and to make the familiar somehow new and exciting. It is your responsibility to interpret and make sense of what is going on for your reader; through your eyes they can vicariously experience the place too.

In particular, it is your ability to accurately describe somewhere and your attention to detail that will give the reader a real sense of the flavour of the place. Yet, in addition to being able to evoke the spirit of the place, you must also give practical, useful information, in case your reader is inspired to pay a visit. Not always an easy balance to achieve but there have to be enough practical suggestions of things to do so that a reader can pick and choose attractions that resonate with them without wasting their valuable time or spending too much money, as well as the more esoteric descriptions.

This need to both evoke and inform at the same time is quite a difficult balancing act to master, but if you read the writings of some of the best travel writers, such as Paul Theroux, Bill Bryson and Tim Cahill, you will soon see how they seamlessly mix the two.

Good preparation

Reading travel books and articles will give you an idea of what works and what does not, plus ways to bring your writing alive. If you are looking to write for a specific publication or website, then make sure you are familiar with their style and their audience. There is no good pitching an idea for luxury dining in Monaco to the *Lonely Planet Guide* editors, just as a feature on hitchhiking through Spain on £5 per day is not going to appeal to *Travel & Leisure*.

If you have your sights set on a general consumer title, you still have to know the rough demographic of the audience. Is it young men, teenage girls or families with young children? What type of features do they usually carry? What can you offer that fits their style? There is so much variety on the news-stands that you are bound to find a publication that is ideal for your feature idea if you look hard enough. Most publications have guidelines available, which tell you how to submit, optimum length of features plus other vital information, and these are worth checking before you pitch your idea to an editor.

If you are gathering material for a book, try to have a theme rather than looking solely at a destination. *The World's Top 100 Backpacker-Friendly Destinations* might be easier to write and more marketable than *A Backpacker's Guide to Monaco*.

Evoking a picture

If you are to successfully bring the essence of a place to life, then you need to provide sensual detail and to paint a picture with your words. Cover all the senses: What food did you eat? How did it taste? What smells assaulted you? How did you feel? What does the place look like? What does it remind you of? Can you hear birdsong or the hubbub of the market? Your goal is to appeal to the reader's senses so that they go on the journey with you.

The other tool in your descriptive armoury is detail. You have to take copious notes when travelling as a writer rather than travelling as a tourist. You must be able to tell the reader how much it costs to get in, when it's busy, how long it has been open, and so on. The reader should want to pack your book or tear out your article and take it with them when they finish reading it; bear in mind when you're writing that it should be helpful, accurate and honest if it is to be a good travel companion.

The most important thing to remember when trying to evoke a picture is that you have to inform as well as evoke; you are aiming for a mix of acute observation, striking description and detailed information, all in your own personal style.

Have an opinion

In travel writing, you should never be afraid to have a point of view. You can freely express your likes and dislikes about a place as long as you can say why. In fact, your personality and preferences need to come through your writing if it is to stand out from other more bland reportage of the locality. A personal tone supported by facts also helps a reader to trust you, just as they might a tour rep when on holiday. As long as you do so with warmth and charm, you can pepper your observations and reporting with your personal take on the place but remember to still be accurate.

Insight – close to home

Don't think that you have to visit exotic locations to be a travel writer. Start by looking with fresh eyes at places closer to home. A feature on a local beauty spot might well appeal to the editor of a national publication who is not familiar with the area.

Good photography

Part of the success of good travel reporting is good photographs to accompany your feature. If you are serious about wanting to get into travel writing, then you might have to think about upgrading your pocket digital camera. You do not need a top of the range SLR digital camera, but you do need to be able to provide good-quality, high-resolution photographs. It probably sounds obvious but, if you are reporting on a wildlife safari in Namibia, you need a camera with a sufficiently powerful zoom so that you can get close-up shots of the wildlife, for example.

Bear in mind that, unless it is exceptionally stunning photography, readers do not want to see buildings and streets. They are simply not that captivating. Take photographs that relate specifically to the things that you talk about in your feature; if there are shots of people who populate your story, so much the better. You can provide captions along with the photographs to explain who and what they are, for example, 'Small pink house on end of promontory where Paulo the fisherman lives'.

If you are submitting to a website, then shoot some brief clips of video to accompany your words. Keep it brief though – a minute of video is too long, as viewers have a very short attention span. A travel writer who can write well and provide good photos/video is definitely ahead of the game.

Find a hook

Most destinations have been written about before on numerous occasions. So try to find a new and original approach to the location and write it from that angle. This will help to catch the reader's attention and is more likely to impress a commissioning editor in the first place.

Specializations

A great way to approach travel writing is through your hobbies or specializations. For example, if you like to paraglide and are quite knowledgeable about the subject, you could write about the top ten bird's-eye-view locations for a specialist magazine. Or perhaps a feature on why Malta is one of the best places in the world to learn to scuba dive could appeal to a men's or women's consumer magazine travel editor. Think about what you have to offer and what value your feature could be to the reader.

I once combined a love of travelling as a family and an interest in mysticism when I pitched an idea for a feature on India about why it is a great destination for families because different cultures and religions can fascinate young children. *Kindred Spirit* magazine, a leading mind, body and spirit title, thought the piece was perfect for their travel slot and the tour company were keen to promote the tours to families, so everyone was happy.

Pitching an idea

When approaching an editor or publisher, it is not enough to let them know that you are about to go on a trip to Prague and would they like something. You have to pitch an idea, and wherever possible, it should be an innovative approach to the place. What can you say to the editor/reader about Prague that has not already been said before?

Once you have your angle, call the publication and get the name and job title of the right person at a magazine, website or newspaper to contact. Then send a personalized email query. Keep it brief and punchy, outlining what your story is about, why it is pertinent to their publication, why it is important to carry the story now and why you are the best person to write it. Your query should be a couple of paragraphs at most – if it is a full page long or more, you need to edit it down.

If you do not hear within a few days, you can send a follow-up email or even call. However, bear in mind that editors are very busy and get hundreds of email queries every day, so be tolerant and polite – and do not take a rejection personally; there are countless reasons why your feature might not be right for that particular publication at this particular time. Take a deep breath and pitch the idea to the next publication on your list.

Insight – personal approach

As a consumer magazine editor, I would sometimes receive feature ideas that had patently been sent out to multiple editors because the font size for my name would be different from the body text of the email. Editors are aware that many writers send out multiple queries, but you are more likely to get a positive response if you at least make an effort to disguise this fact.

New media

The explosion of blogs, online magazines and online communities means that there are more opportunities than ever for travel writers and realistically, this new media arena probably represents the best opportunity for a would-be travel writer to get your work out there. Check out travel websites and subscribe to the outlet's newsletter or RSS feed so that you know precisely what they want, what they are currently purchasing and how to format it. You can then tailor your feature ideas to their goals.

You can start modestly on the social network sites such as Facebook, YouTube, Flicker, Travelistic, LinkedIn and Twitter, by putting up stories, photos and videos (having already edited out any silly drunken snaps) to show potential editors and to publicize your work. Alternatively, you could create a blog as a showcase for your writing talents, link to your favourite travel sites and, if they are impressed, they could well link back.

Who knows where it could lead? Eventually, you could collect your travel writings together to form the basis of a travel book.

TRAVEL WRITING EXERCISES

Exercise one

One of the greatest assets of the travel writer is being able to look at the world in a new way, and that is the focus of this first exercise.

▶ Pick a location close to your home – it could even be your home town or village.
▶ Write a short travel feature describing your location, designed to intrigue and excite someone who has never been there before.
▶ Keep it brief – say 450 words – but remember to include the vital ingredients of good travel writing; namely sensual descriptive appeal, personal input, detail and information.
▶ When you are happy with your feature, if at all possible, why not send it to a friend who has never visited your chosen spot and then invite them to come and stay, to see if the description lives up to the reality.

Exercise two

The best way to evoke a place or memory is to use descriptive language that appeals to the senses.

▶ Write a short description of a place that made an impact on you. It does not have to be a holiday destination – it could be a famous house you visited, a lakeside view or a particularly welcoming pub.
▶ Try to describe the spot or the event using language that evokes the sights, sounds, smells and feel of the occasion. For example, if it was a memorable night at a pub on Exmoor, what conversations did you overhear at the bar? Was the stone flagging wet from walkers' boots? Did the pub grub smell delicious or did the smell of grease make you nauseous? How did the velour stools feel after a long hike?

12

Writing for magazines and newspapers

In this chapter you will learn:
- *how to pitch ideas to editors*
- *where to find ideas*
- *how to write articles*.

Magazines and newspapers have been cutting the numbers of in-house staff during the economic downturn. In fact, the number of mainstream UK journalism jobs has shrunk by between 27–33 per cent over the last decade to around 40,000, according to a University of Central Lancashire report. The upside of this trend, however, is that the print media has been forced to rely more and more on contributions from freelance writers and, as a result, the market for non-fiction articles is buoyant at the moment. Even in brighter economic times, most magazines use at least a couple of freelancers, so there is always some freelance work available.

Add to this the fact that the breadth of magazine topics is huge, ranging from specialist hobbyist magazines and trade journals to consumer titles and newspapers, and you can see why this is a good genre for new writers.

Finding an outlet

Realistically, it is exceptionally hard to break into writing for the glossy news-stand magazine titles as the market is extremely competitive. Nonetheless, if you aim your sights a little lower, there are plenty of magazines that rely on a mixture of contributions from professional writers and from their readers. These reader-contributors to hobbyist titles often have an enormous amount of specialist knowledge to share, so editors tend to forgive them if their writing is lacking in finesse. It therefore follows that if you can supply a well-written article that is superior in style to the usual offerings, yet still informative you stand a good chance of acceptance by these specialist magazines.

If you want to find out more about which magazines are being published, there are two main guides that writers use: the *Writers' and Artists' Yearbook* and *The Writers' Handbook*, both of which are published annually and are available from bookshops. These are useful to writers as they provide helpful information about hundreds of magazines and newspapers, but that still leaves thousands of trade magazines, and in-house and flight publications to consider, not to mention local and free newspapers – none of which are covered in the writers' guides. For contact details for all these additional media outlets, try *Benns UK Media Directory*, *Willings Press Guide* and the *Guardian Media Guide*, all of which can be found in local libraries.

Writing for national newspapers is just as competitive and cut-throat as writing for national magazines, if not more so. Therefore, it is probably worth cutting your teeth on local and regional newspapers. They have to fill their pages on a daily or weekly basis, so there is ample scope for the novice writer. Think about reporting on local events, interviewing local celebrities, craftsmen or artists, writing reviews for restaurants or plays, or covering local sports events. Perhaps you have a local history story that might be of interest.

Normally, features for newspapers are time-sensitive, so you must pitch ideas in advance to the appropriate editor – larger-circulation newspapers may have different editors for specific areas such as sport, features, arts and politics. Send a succinct email outlining your idea, as these are extremely busy people. If s/he expresses interest, you can always go into greater detail in a phone call. If an editor is reluctant to commission you (they tend to prefer journalists with a proven track record), you could always submit a couple of examples of the sort of reviews or features you have in mind, together with a covering letter.

Getting started

If you tick most of the following boxes, then perhaps you are a prime candidate to be writing for magazines and newspapers:

- ▶ I have no problems coming up with lots of ideas
- ▶ I can write to length
- ▶ I can meet a deadline
- ▶ I can interview people.

If there are any of the above areas where you think you might be a little shaky, here are some hints and tips that should help.

COMING UP WITH FEATURE IDEAS

Your world

All around you and probably every day of your life, you can find countless sources of inspiration for magazine and newspaper articles. It is simply a matter of changing how you view your own world. You have to have an enquiring mind. Are you interested in the stories that you hear from colleagues and family? Is there an aspect of your chosen hobby that could interest a wider audience? Are you entering a new stage of family life and have some insight into this phase that could interest other parents? Perhaps a local event merits a review in the local paper?

These particular suggestions may not apply directly to you but you can see that for each idea, you are drawing straight from the wealth of feature material that exists in your everyday life and from your circle of family, colleagues and friends.

Reading magazines and newspapers

Alternatively, you can start from the finished product and work back. Pick up magazines and newspapers and look at the types of articles that they carry regularly and then try to come up with ideas to fill these regular pages. For example, I am a regular contributor to *Kindred Spirit* magazine. It carries a regular feature called 'Words of Wisdom' in which a notable or interesting figure from the mind, body and spirit world talks about things that are important to them, or that they have learnt during their professional and private lives or about events that have shaped their lives. One page is devoted to this slot in every issue. Supposing you were familiar with the magazine, and you met someone interesting who fits the bill, why not interview them, with this feature in mind? You could then try to sell your idea to the editor, who would probably be impressed by the fact that you have targeted a specific regular feature of the magazine.

Seasonal events

Another rich supply of feature ideas can be found in annual seasonal events such as Christmas and New Year, Halloween, Easter, Harvest Festival, Guy Fawkes Night, and summer and winter solstice. You have to pitch ideas that relate to seasonal events well in advance as magazines are commissioning as much as six months in advance, although a lead-in time of three to four months is more common. It is also important to be inventive, since editors are inundated with articles on such seasonal subjects, but the good news is that there is always a demand.

When editing a consumer women's magazine, it was virtually compulsory that we would carry some sort of beauty feature on sun protection in June, an article about cold and flu prevention in the Autumn and, in the lead-up to Christmas, the issue was brimming with festive features. It is hard for editors to keep this cyclical material fresh and interesting for readers, so any innovative spin you can put on your feature idea would undoubtedly be well received.

Insight – get to know a magazine

If you look at a magazine's contents page or occasionally at the running strap line at the top of the page, you can soon see which type of features the magazine carries in every issue (some are even listed under regulars on the contents page). You can then come up with feature ideas to pitch directly at that specific spot.

WRITING TO LENGTH

If you are sending a feature to a magazine on spec, then it is crucial that it fits into the space allocation usually given to that type of article. For example, there is no point in sending a 1,500-word review of a local theatre production if the published reviews usually run at around 500 words. It could be the best-written review ever, but if it requires an editor to spend an afternoon subbing the piece down by two-thirds, it is unlikely to be accepted.

Magazine features are most commonly commissioned to fill one page (about 750 words), two pages (about 1,500 words) or three pages (about 2,250 words), so it is worth getting used to writing articles that roughly conform to these lengths. When editing magazines, I would routinely receive unsolicited articles of anywhere between 4,500–7,000 words. It does not matter how gripping the material or how well written, these submissions were almost invariably rejected, so make sure you either write to length or that you edit your work down to a more suitable feature length before submission.

MEETING DEADLINES

Given enough time, most keen writers can produce a well-crafted article but, when the chips are down, can you write a publishable 1,500-word feature by Friday? Before you submit a feature idea to an editor, you must be confident that you can write your proposed article by the date given. This is a fundamental requirement if you are going to write regularly for any sort of periodicals.

INTERVIEWING PEOPLE

Whether you interview a local sculpture who is about to host an exhibition for your regional newspaper, or a business leader for a feature in a financial trade journal, being able to interview people face-to-face or over the phone is a simple process that you need to master. Here are some tips:

- ▶ Make initial contact by email with the interviewee to set up the interview.
- ▶ If you are meeting in person, then dress appropriately for the setting.
- ▶ Always be punctual.
- ▶ Put your interviewee at ease with some easy chit chat, but not for too long.
- ▶ Conduct the interview using pre-prepared questions.
- ▶ Be prepared to follow the conversation if the interviewee veers off at a tangent but, if it is not leading anywhere interesting, gently draw them back to your pre-determined questions.
- ▶ If you are interviewing someone about their latest book, it helps to have read it.
- ▶ If your subject is well known or in the public eye, it is useful to have some background information on them (celebrities and authors will often have a publicist who is only too happy to provide you with background information; otherwise the internet and newspaper cuttings are a good start).
- ▶ Let the interviewee know that you will be recording the conversation but you may want to take notes just in case technology lets you down or to underscore key points in your mind.

What kind of feature?

There are so many different categories of feature writing that it would be impossible to list them all here. However the following list covers the most common approaches, some of which might dovetail well with your areas of interest or expertise.

'HOW TO' OR SELF-HELP

These are the bread and butter of specialist, hobbyist and women's magazines. They range from the practical such as 'How to prune roses' or 'How to wear eyeliner', to the more sociological and/or pseudo-psychological, which run along the lines of 'How to communicate with your teenager' or 'How to get over the death of a loved one'. Not only are these types of features prolific but you will often see them as cover lines on the front cover of magazines because they catch the reader's attention on the shelves.

Usually, a 'how to' article comprises a brief and upbeat introduction followed by more practical information. If it is an entirely practical 'how to' you may well offer step-by-step bulleted or numbered instructions within the text. The golden rule for all 'how to' or self-help articles is that the advice or instructions should be easy to understand and follow, and should work. Delia Smith has staked her not inconsiderable reputation on the fact that readers know her recipes will turn out well. If you are supplying advice about your chosen craft or hobby, you must be equally sure that the process will produce a good end result.

MOTIVATIONAL

Newspaper and magazine editors love a 'triumph over adversity' story because they are upbeat and they generate sales. They are especially popular with the tabloid newspapers and downmarket women's magazines, particularly if the tone is one of 'I'm a regular guy and if I can do it, anyone can'. You may have your own inspirational tale to tell or perhaps you know of someone who has had a remarkable experience that could inspire others. These real-life stories could form the basis of a feature idea to pitch to an editor.

Of course, if you draw on your personal experiences, they do not have to be motivational. You could simply be reporting about something that has happened in your life or to someone close to you. Stories about carers are hugely popular at the moment, as is anything to do with health and education.

TRAVEL

I don't want to burst anyone's bubble but if you think that you are going to persuade a travel editor to send you to an exotic location all-expenses-paid in return for a 1,500-word feature, you are going to be sorely disappointed. Travel writing is a highly competitive market (see Chapter 11).

That said, I know of a writer who got their first published work after sending a review of their adventure holiday to the travel company, who then published it in their brochure. This tends to be the exception rather than the rule though, so rather than concentrating on overseas travel, why not think about writing a travel feature about your own locality and sending it to a national magazine.

SPECIALIST

If you have a background in social work, psychotherapy, allopathic health or complementary therapies, then you have specialist knowledge that could shed light on other people's health or relationship problems, and this is a regular and popular topic in magazines and newspapers.

FILLERS

Although the name sounds slightly disparaging, fillers for magazines are an often-overlooked way into the world of published non-fiction. As the name suggests, fillers are small items that are used to break up longer features and can include:

▶ letters
▶ gaffes, such as reporting the funny things that people say
▶ humorous anecdotes
▶ handy hints.

Admittedly, writing fillers is not the prestige end of the non-fiction market, but magazines often pay handsomely *pro rata* for fillers, and it can be a way to get you known by an editor, so acting as a springboard to greater things. Not to mention the fact that seeing your name in print can be a huge boost to your confidence.

Insight – be realistic

Opinion pieces and observational columns are great fun to write and very popular in both magazines and newspapers but, sadly, if you submit this genre of article, it is unlikely to be published unless you are a celebrity or a named writer.

The above list of feature categories is by no means exhaustive and if you should come across others in your reading and research that strike you as possibilities, by all means give them a go.

Difficult fields to crack

The following categories of feature exist but you may have difficulties finding a market for them.

Consumer testing: also known as service pieces, where products are compared for various criteria such as value for money, looks, efficiency, and so on. These are almost invariably written by in-house journalists.

Nostalgic features: although there is a growing demand, editors are inundated with nostalgic features about the good old days from older readers, and the vast majority are rejected.

Opinion: a magazine or newspaper column is almost invariably written by well-known journalists or celebrities.

Humour: there are fewer and fewer outlets for humorous writing. Better to enliven your general features with some wit rather than expressly setting out to sell a humorous feature.

Researching your idea

Once you have a feature idea and you've identified what sort of article you want to write, you will need to do some preliminary research to make sure the idea is substantive enough to support a 1,500 word article. If there appears to be plenty to say or something new to describe, then it is worth researching in greater detail. The best sources for research material include:

- reference books
- back issues of periodicals, available in libraries
- public records
- the internet (but make sure the web page source is reliable)
- publicity departments of governing and professional bodies
- embassies and national travel information services (for overseas information)
- interviewing specialists in the field.

Once you have collected together all the necessary information for your article, start to sort through and collate the material into different areas. I find lever arch files or box files are best for keeping data safely together. I also use reporter notebooks for making handwritten notes to myself on the subject. I store these together with the research material once the feature is finished; you just never know when it may come in handy and it is useful if a sub-editor has any queries prior to going to print.

Writing an article

Now you are ready to write your article. You will have your own personal style but there are a few basics to remember when structuring and writing your feature.

Make an initial impact The opening paragraph is important as it has to capture the editor's imagination and inspire him or her to keep reading the rest of the feature, so make it interesting, shocking, funny or compelling in some way.

Looking good Layout is important. Using sub-headings and side-bars/boxes to introduce new ideas and to break up large swathes of text helps the reader to stay interested. Present your work typed double-spaced, with text aligned left but not right, and with the first sentence of each section ranged left and subsequent paragraphs indented.

Writing tips Do not allow your writing to become flabby, which effectively means keeping the sentences and paragraphs short, vocabulary simple and use of adjectives and adverbs to a minimum. In 1946, George Orwell prescribed the following rules of good writing and they still apply today.

- ▶ Never use a metaphor, simile or other figure of speech that you are used to seeing in print.
- ▶ Never use a long word where a short one will do.
- ▶ If it is possible to cut a word out, always cut it out.
- ▶ Never use the passive where you can use the active.
- ▶ Never use a foreign phrase, a scientific word or a jargon word if you can think of an everyday English equivalent.
- ▶ Break any of these rules sooner than say anything outright barbarous.

Facts, anecdotes and quotations All can be a valuable addition to a magazine article but you must make sure the provenance is reliable and that they are accurate – a sub-editor may well check.

Length Writing to length is crucial. Do not get carried away and end up writing way too much.

Tone You will be guided by the style of your target magazine, but as a general rule of thumb, you should be aiming for an informative, relaxed, conversational style that makes the magazine reader feel comfortable.

Final edit Before submitting your article, make sure you proofread it thoroughly and cast a final eye over it to check that it is a taut as possible; not too wordy, with a relaxed tone, informative without sounding like a textbook.

Pitching to an editor

Selling a feature idea to a magazine or newspaper editor is known as 'a pitch'. Once you have come up with an idea and done some initial background research regarding its viability, you are then in a position to approach the relevant editor of your target publication to see if you can get them to commission you to write the piece. This is undoubtedly harder if you do not have any published work to date, but not impossible. Usually, a journalist will pitch ideas by phone, email or letter but I suggest you avoid using the phone until you have a proven track record; an editor is more likely to read your written proposal without interruption, whereas on the phone, s/he is likely to ask who else you have written for at the beginning of the conversation and you may not be given a chance to sell yourself.

If you are emailing or writing to an editor, you have just one chance to persuade them, so you had better make it count. Make sure you give consideration to the following points if you want your pitch to be successful.

Correct name and title
Get the name and title of the relevant editor and address them directly. For example, you want the features editor to consider a general article but, if you are writing about 'Ten ways to improve your Victoria Sandwich', you should approach the cookery editor.

Catchy title
Not absolutely essential, but this is a good way of encapsulating the essence of the feature and helps the editor picture how it might work on the page.

Why this article?
Before you outline the idea for your article, you can briefly explain some background information plus the specific angle that your feature might take and how it might benefit the reader. For example, for a feature on children's eyesight that I wrote for *The Times*, my pitch quoted statistics on the number of children with eyesight problems, explained how this goes largely undetected because parents do not take up the offer of free eye tests and outlined what readers should do to make sure their children's eyesight was fine. I also had a first-hand case study to help sway the argument.

Why this author?
There is no shortage of writers pitching feature ideas. You need to succinctly point out that you are the right person to write this particular article because of your expertise/knowledge/qualifications. If you have relevant cuttings, you can attach them or enclose copies with your pitch. If not, you do not have to draw attention to your lack of experience.

Peg or hook
In magazine and newspaper publishing, editors are always looking for what is called a peg or hook to hang a feature on. This could be an anniversary; for example, there were countless articles published from every conceivable angle ranging from Spitfires and dogfights to women pilots and downed aviators around the time of the 70th anniversary of the Battle of Britain in 2010. Dates and anniversaries are obvious hooks to look out for but events in the public arena can also be useful pegs on which to pitch an idea. I sold a feature on

allowing our children more freedom to play using the peg of new Government guidelines for teachers taking kids on school trips that was about to be published.

Deciding on a peg can be something of a 'chicken and egg' situation. Perhaps you know of an anniversary that is coming up which triggers a feature idea, or maybe you have a feature in mind and then try to find a hook to hang it on. Whichever way around, it is important that you give yourself and the editors you approach plenty of time before the anniversary or event, since magazines in particular have long lead times, plus you may not get an acceptance from the first magazine or newspaper you approach.

Double-check
Do not steel yourself to pitch an idea by email or letter and then dash it off in such a hurry that it contains mistakes. You have one chance and one chance only with this editor, so it is important to make a good impression. To this end, check and double-check your message for spelling and grammatical errors, make sure the layout is clear and, if it is a letter, that you have not used more than one sheet of paper.

Unsolicited submissions
If you perpetually come up against a brick wall when you pitch ideas because you have no proven track record, you might be able to get around this by writing a feature specifically for a magazine and sending it to the appropriate editor with a covering letter and accompanying stamped, self-addressed envelope (SAE). In fact, while you are waiting for a reply, why not write another article for another magazine and send that one in too, so that you increase your chances of acceptance from one or other magazine.

If you have not heard back in around six weeks, you could give a brief call or send an email to enquire. Although some features will undoubtedly be returned – perhaps with a brief rejection note, perhaps not – one may be taken up by an interested editor and then you will have published work for when you pitch the next idea.

Insight – beware of multi-targeting
Some writers pitch the same feature idea to several magazines at the same time but this can lead to problems. I recommend approaching one magazine at a time. If you favour the simultaneous approach, target magazines in different markets so that you can specifically tailor the article for each title if the idea is accepted by more than one editor.

JOURNALISM EXERCISE

▶ Choose a magazine or local newspaper that you know well and decide on a regular feature slot that you think you could contribute to.

▶ Research and write your feature to the required length using the editorial tips outlined in this chapter.

▶ Put your feature to one side and revisit it the following day.

▶ On re-reading the feature, candidly assess whether or not you would have continued to read it if you had seen it in the magazine. If the answer is 'Yes', then why not submit it to the relevant editor? If the answer is 'No', then perhaps some further editing or rewriting is required.

13

Writing for children

In this chapter you will learn:
- *how to make your writing age appropriate*
- *the importance of good research*
- *how to know what sells*
- *ways to offer additional benefits to your words.*

There used to be an unspoken belief in publishing circles that children's non-fiction was somehow the poor relation of literature. It rarely received reviews and, sad to say, expectations of authors were low. In fact, writing for children's non-fiction was often dull and frequently uninspiring. Thankfully, things have changed in recent years, and children's non-fiction is no longer looked down upon. Quite the contrary, in fact, as non-fiction titles are now among the hottest-selling books for children. In 2009, the children's, young adult and education non-fiction genre grew by 4.5 per cent in value terms, according to the Nielsen Book Market Trends report. In part, this is due to a sea-change in publishers' and authors' aspirations. Today, the aim is to inspire and inform children, rather than lecture them, and this has resulted in some brilliant non-fiction books for children. No longer is it enough to believe that if you present the information, it will inevitably be understood. Fact is not necessarily meaning. Authors now have to think not only about what they write but how they present the information.

And the good news is that kids have an insatiable curiosity; they love to know things, so the future for good non-fiction writing looks assured. You might fancy writing non-fiction for children, if you can:

▶ write well
▶ have an enquiring mind

- ▶ can research accurately
- ▶ can write to deadlines.

The best news is that this is one of the least competitive niches of the writing market, and there are publishers looking for new authors.

Knowing your market

Non-fiction writing for children is an umbrella term that covers a wide range of genres. It comprises subjects ranging from history, science and biography, through art, 'how to' and craft books to sports, survival and activities books. And these categories can be narrowed down into greater specialism, so that within the activity book category, you might include holiday or museum books, for example. The list is endless.

Non-fiction for children is one of the few genres where publishers not only welcome original ideas and proposals, but some are even looking for writers to fulfil assignments for them, although admittedly, the requirement is almost certainly going to be for an agented writer with a proven track record. Nonetheless, the market is relatively buoyant, and most publishers will consider proposals and ideas, especially those publishers who specialize in books for the school and library market. Obviously, these book ideas are often driven by the changing school curriculum, but there are openings for new books for children ranging from pre-schoolers and emergent readers to the more complex and in-depth issues covered in books for secondary school students.

There is also a growing market in writing non-fiction for children's magazines and websites, and this can be more lucrative than writing books. These freelance opportunities range from contributions to simple club magazines to glossy on-the-shelf mountain biking magazines and e-zines.

Before you start

The first prerequisite for writing for children is an enthusiasm for your subject. You do not necessarily have to have an in-depth knowledge – good research can overcome that obstacle – but a passion that translates onto the page is an essential.

As you have already seen, the range of topics is wide open, so whatever you are interested in – whether it is as huge as space exploration or as unusual as *feng shui* for a teenager's bedroom – it is all viable. What you need is to take the topic in a new direction – that is what editors are really looking for. And do not be afraid to narrow down your topic. Rather than looking at World War I, you could look at the microcosm of stretcher-bearers in World War I, for example, and tell your young audience something new and interesting about them. The most basic information in some detail can be interesting to children.

Insight – be versatile

My agent once put me forward to write a kids' non-fiction book on cryptozoology (the study of creatures whose existence has not been substantiated). I couldn't claim to be an expert on the subject but the publisher knew me to be a thorough researcher. I got the commission and I have to say, I really enjoyed writing this book and now consider myself to be quite knowledgeable on this unusual subject.

MARKET RESEARCH

There is little point in investing time and energy in thoroughly researching and writing your book if there is no market for this particular topic. So check out what is currently on the market or on publishers' lists to see if your idea holds water.

AGE-RELATED

Once you have identified your topic and satisfied yourself that there is a market for such a book, you must decide which age range you are going to target. Children's books are roughly broken down into five categories:

1 **Picture books** which are appropriate for readers aged approximately zero to three years old, although some children's non-fiction publishers are happy to take picture books, where the illustrations play as important a role as the text in telling the story, up to an older age range, say eight years old.
2 **Early reader books**, aka 'easy readers', are for children aged five to eight, who are just starting to read on their own. They are often designed to help a child to expand his or her vocabulary and reading skills.
3 **Chapter books,** for ages seven to ten. These books have short chapters and still have relatively short paragraphs for the younger readers. However longer chapter books are available

for ages nine to twelve, that tackle more sophisticated themes and cover topics such as biographies, science, history and multicultural themes.

4 **Young adult**, which are predominantly for 12-year-olds and upwards, often covering topics that are pertinent to today's tweenies and teenagers. They are aimed at children who have outgrown the chapter books but are not yet ready for subjects that 15-year-olds and upwards might read.

5 However, a sub-category seems to be forming within young adult non-fiction. In the late 1990s, I was asked to write a survival guide series (under the pen name Rory Storm) to interest this new age category. The books were specifically targeted at **boys**, aged between 10 and 14 years old, and it was hoped that such titles would prevent boys from disaffecting from reading as they so often do at this age. In fact, the series did exceptionally well, especially in America.

Insight – not as easy as it looks

People think that writing for very young children must be easy because there are so few words but in fact it is extremely difficult. If you want to try to write for this market, for guidance, look at the books that booksellers or librarians recommended for this age group, as they know what works.

WRITING APPROACH

Finally, you have to decide whether you are going to write your book as a straightforward non-fiction title or whether you are going to embrace the currently popular style of 'narrative non-fiction' or 'creative non-fiction'. If this does not mean much to you, take a look at Chapter 7, or try taking a look at the fantasy-style *Magic School Bus* science books or Scholastic's *Double Take* non-fiction series for 12 years and up. For younger children, the *Explorers Wanted* series written by Simon Chapman is a good example of these narrative non-fiction books that read like well-written short stories but are actually factual. Some of the best children's books use this approach to bring historical events and characters to life or to explain scientific phenomena in an accessible and exciting way.

Learn your subject

To be a successful non-fiction writer for children, you must firstly be a thorough and skilled researcher. You do not have to be an expert in the field – after all most authors who write about climbing Everest have not reached the summit of the highest mountain in the world. Publishers prefer to commission someone who is able to research a topic and who possesses the special skills needed to write for children rather than an expert who cannot write.

Whatever you do, avoid the temptation to rely on a few tired facts from old books or the internet because 'You are just writing for kids'. If you skimp on the research, your book will be superficial and uninteresting. Here are a few tips to help you to research effectively.

Use reliable sources By all means use current newspapers, books and magazines as you start to search but then check the sources quoted by the author in footnotes, bibliographies and references and read those too. You are aiming to find primary sources such as published research papers for each piece of information you plan to use. Journals and diaries are excellent primary sources for biographical research, for example.

In addition, if you can interview a specialist in the field, that can be invaluable. Whether you are writing about go-karting or heart surgery, interviewing a champion driver or a leading cardiologist or heart research scientist is a great way to get answers to your questions and to make sense of things. They may even be willing to check what you have written for technical accuracy. Be wary of internet sources since anyone can set up a website and post uncorroborated information.

Check and double-check All facts must be checked and rechecked. Make sure you have multiple reliable sources wherever possible.

Throw your net wide The strange thing about research is that you never know where it is going to lead you. If you follow the trail from one source to the next, it will invariably turn up something interesting. So read everything!

Make a note of quirky facts Kids are absolutely fascinated by quirky facts – you can never have too many, so never pass one by.

Accept help University and research libraries will often open their doors to writers and they have wonderful resources, not least of which is a librarian who has specialist research skills. If a librarian is willing to help you to trawl their treasure trove of research journals, microfilm and microfiche files, special collections and online databases, be gracious and accept immediately.

If you have researched your book thoroughly, you will have mountains of information but you do not have to include all of it. As you re-read all your research, certain key points will jump out at you. These are the messages that you want your reader to remember, so group your information around these important facts and eliminate less relevant items – but do not discard them completely.

Whether you keep your work electronically or in paper files, keep everything together. In this way, you can refer back whenever you want. Who knows, something that seemed irrelevant at the first edit might make a useful fact box or sidebar at a later date. Once you have the essentials of your research information, it can be useful to write the core themes of the book on separate index cards and then code each piece of research according to one of these themes. In that way, an outline for the format or chapters of the book may well become apparent.

Write entertainingly for kids

Writing for children is not easy. You have to impart a great deal of information in a small number of words. And, in today's world, you must make your text exciting and compelling enough to compete with the ubiquitous appeal of television's cable channels and computer CD-ROMs.

Fundamentally, good non-fiction writers for children remember what it was like to be a child and retain that sense of wonder and amazement at the world around them. If you have this gift, then your book will almost certainly resonate well with a young audience, but there are also other techniques that you can bear in mind when writing for children that can be of benefit.

WRITING STYLE

Although the principal aim of a non-fiction book is to impart knowledge, there is no reason why it should be dull or boring in any way. To successfully grab a child's attention, your writing style should be lively and engaging.

Essentially, you are looking for ways to bring the subject to life, whether it is science, history or a hobby. A biography of a prominent figure does not need to be a chronology of his or her life, listing dates and key events, rather it can be full of anecdotes that show what kind of a person they were. Similarly, in the past, history books were often a dry list of dates, coronations and battles, which left many young readers uninspired. Today, you can bring history to life by looking at real, ordinary people and painting a picture of everyday life in extraordinary and unfamiliar times. Exceptional events can then stand out in context and by contrast.

For younger audiences, it can be useful to tap into their love of the weird, unusual or frankly gross aspects of your subject. So rather than saying that a hippo's mouth has one of the widest gapes in the natural world, why not conjure up an image, saying 'If you are up to four feet tall, you could stand in a hippo's mouth when he yawns and not even have to bend your head!' This young readership responds well to a breathless excitement in the tone of your writing, which is infectious and compelling. You can be as amazed and excited as they are by what you are writing.

For boys, who often find reading harder and stop reading sooner than girls, non-fiction is frequently their preferred choice of reading material. If you decide to specifically target boys, then try to give your book an exciting narrative thread that pulls it all together rather than making it an unrelated fact-gathering exercise for the reader, and you will maintain their attention from cover to cover.

Whatever the age or gender of your audience, you have to grab their attention from the outset because this computer-literate generation have a low boredom threshold and will not be patient for long. Get to the point straightaway, and keep your writing rich and interesting with the use of humour, sharp detail and good observation backed up by solid research.

In terms of writing tone, it is hard to strike a good balance. Certainly, children are more savvy and streetwise than we were at the same age, so it can be worth reading books aimed at a specific age group in order to recognize the appropriate tone. More importantly, children can spot if you are patronizing them, so avoid being too sweet or jaunty. Conversely, they do not want to be lectured either. If they sense any condescension or that you are talking down to them, they will feel insulted and immediately abandon your book, irrespective of how informative it may be.

However, the cardinal sin of a children's non-fiction author is to moralize. You are not writing a cheesy Disney script, so do not be tempted to slip a sermonizing message into your text. Your average ten-year-old will spot it immediately and, in all likelihood, give up. Of course, if there is a lesson to be learned, include it by all means, but observe the principal rule of all writing and show it, don't tell it.

One of the hardest parts of writing for children is paring the words down to the exciting essentials. If you struggle with this, it may help to ask yourself 'What is the most important point?' and focus on that. If you have two or more points that are equally important, then the way to decide is to question which point has most child appeal or is the more exciting, and go with that one.

Finally, your writing must be accurate. A publisher will not welcome a string of phone calls or letters from irate parents saying that a particular recipe in a kids' cookery book does not work, or a formula in a popular science book is wrong. So make sure the facts in your book are accurate and that any step-by-step instructions in a 'how to' book actually work. This means following your written procedure without using any initiative, simply following the directions, and seeing if it works out. Even if you have gleaned the activity from another book, do not assume that it has been thoroughly tested. Always double-check the instructions yourself or enlist the help of a young volunteer.

Insight – fail-safe instructions

When I wrote the six Survival Guides for Boys and *The Curious Girl's Book of Adventure*, I would get my sons to follow the 'how to' instructions without interfering. If there were directions that were ambiguous or they didn't understand, I would rewrite them until they could follow them without help. They loved making survival shelters and reluctantly became quite proficient at weaving paper baskets.

LANGUAGE

The language you use when writing for children has to be interesting and lyrical, yet readily understandable. Obviously, you have to choose age-appropriate language for your audience, but it must also be laid out and constructed so facts and information are easily accessible and understood. And you should never underestimate how hard and time consuming it can be to translate complex ideas and information into words that children can understand. However, when it comes together, it is hugely rewarding. Writing for pre-school children (five and under) is probably the most challenging in terms of language because you only have a few words to put on each page. You have to be able to explain a concept in a quarter of the number of words that you might use for older children, so you must choose every word very carefully. Each word must be just right and make sense, and must also have a rhythm that helps them to work together as a whole.

All children, whatever their age, are more sophisticated nowadays, so getting the tone/language right for the reading age and still managing to avoid talking down to them is the goal you are trying to achieve.

Just as writing for the very young holds its own specific challenges, so too does writing for the older child – more specifically, credibility issues. Adults using slang, jargon or street talk sound phony – or as my sons might say 'sad'. Avoid talking in the vernacular. Instead use the same language as you would usually but keep it 'real', showing your genuine passion for the subject. You cannot fake this. If you pretend to care about something that is outside your realm of experience, it will be clear to the reader. A savvy 14-year-old will be able to spot if you have no snowboarding knowledge or experience, even if you rave about the sport. Here are a few more ideas that might help you to successfully select the right words and tone when writing for children.

▶ Have fun with language. You can spice up your text by using onomatopoeia, alliteration, homonyms, double entendres, humour and rhyme.
▶ Use examples from the child's world to help them to understand complex ideas or information.
▶ Use similes and metaphors, for example, 'A flea can jump up to 30 cm, that's 20 times as long as its own body.' Or compare sizes to something familiar so the child has a point of reference, for example, 'A giant squid has the largest eyes of any animal – at 39 cm across, it is 16 times wider than a human eye.' Just make sure your points of reference are relevant to today's children – for example, most will have no idea what a LP is.
▶ Build a conspiratorial bond with your reader by being friendly and talking directly to the individual. Involve him or her by using an informal conversational style, for example, 'Bet you didn't see that coming!'

- ▶ Ask questions.
- ▶ Vary sentence length.
- ▶ As this is non-fiction, stick to the facts. But there is nothing to stop you bringing the child into your world by using the second person, for example, 'Imagine a fire broke out in your school. You would have to keep cool and act fast.'

FORMATS

How you frame and present your information can be almost as important as what you write when it comes to children's non-fiction. Just as you have to keep your writing rich and interesting, so you want to make the format of your book exciting and involving too. It is now widely recognized that children learn in different ways – some are auditory learners, some are visual and some are kinaesthetic, so using different approaches and tools within your book, and even to support it (ancillary content), can help to broaden its appeal. Here are some ideas:

Sidebars

As children are not keen on hunting too hard to find the information they need, most commonly, this involves introducing sidebars, glossaries and highlighted fact boxes and so on, to help to make the information accessible. These devices can also help you to keep your word count down, since children, especially early readers, are more likely to finish a shorter chapter.

Interactive

If you can incorporate an interactive approach that provides plenty for the reader to do, it can encourage children to explore and investigate on their own. By this, I mean supplementary content such as blank pages dedicated to a children's journal, some discovery activities or an additional parents' guide, can all keep children involved. For example, a book on British native trees could encourage a child to collect a leaf and draw it on the open space provided, or a geology book might suggest an experiment that the child could perform on a certain type of rock, and then the child can record the results on the data page provided.

Gift boxes

You may well have seen the plethora of what are called gift box books on the shelves, especially coming up to Christmas. These gift boxes include a book and then a couple of items that relate to the subject; a book on candle making might be packaged with a small mould and a bag of wax granules and a couple of wicks. If you can come up with a suggestion for how your book might fit into this gift book category, you could make it a more appealing proposition to a publisher or book packager who specializes in these types of products.

Activities

Publishers are very receptive to children's non-fiction books that include activities. A practical exercise that contains a list of equipment and step-by-step instructions is the most common approach but you can simply include practical suggestions within the body text – it only takes a couple of sentences to explain something along the lines of, 'If you make your finger wet and then run it around the rim of a glass, it will make a humming noise.'

Another way to interact with your young reader is to include quizzes and questionnaires – kids love to fill these in. Or why not turn the whole book into a mystery that has to be solved by the reader? Perhaps you could suggest a completely different physical format for your book. Educational and library publishers sometimes produce books that can be as big as 2½ feet tall as these large format books are ideal to share with one or more child or to show in front of the class.

Insight – photographic sources

I have found that experts are often happy to give you access to their original photographic material for publication, especially if you have interviewed them or quoted them in the book.

Illustrations

Most children's books, irrespective of target age, rely heavily on clear illustrations and photography, especially crafts, cookery and 'how to' books. As the writer, you are not expected to provide or commission these illustrations, but if you see something suitable during your research, then you can suggest this to a potential publisher/editor, who often welcomes fresh sources for illustrations. Once the book is commissioned and in the production process, you should work very closely with the editor and illustrator/photographer, because there is nothing worse than an illustration in a book that wrongly depicts the steps of an activity. And this is never truer than with a book for children.

Internet links

A more recent development in children's non-fiction is the link with the internet in books. Some non-fiction books, like Usborne's internet-linked *Encyclopaedia of the Ancient World*, contains internet links unobtrusively placed in the text so that the reader has further opportunities to explore ideas via the Usborne website where they can find an animation of Vesuvius erupting, or a video of polar bears, for example. This connection between children's books and internet support is still in its infancy, but an astute writer could bear this development in mind when compiling a synopsis for a non-fiction book proposal.

Promoting your book

The best children's non-fiction relies on two key elements, namely illustrations that are visually eye-catching and writing that stimulates and excites. If both elements are structured in such a way as to aid children's understanding, then you have a successful young non-fiction book, and you will be in demand. In my experience, today's children's publishers and writers are committed to producing non-fiction books that can enlighten, interest and excite young readers, and hopefully 'foster a spirit of enquiry', to quote an apt if well-worn phrase. And with this aim in mind, do not be surprised if, having published your book, you are invited to appear in local schools and libraries, and even book festivals, to talk about your subject. Such is the current enthusiasm among publishers, teachers and librarians to reach children who might not otherwise come across a book that captures their imagination.

Therefore, not only is it critical to have enthusiasm for your subject because that conveys itself through your writing to the children, but also because you may well be publicizing your book and its subject matter for some time after its publication.

WRITING FOR CHILDREN EXERCISE

▶ Write 750 words on one of your favourite hobbies for an audience of 8-year-olds.
▶ Try to ensure that the reader comes away with a clear understanding of what you do, how you do it and why.
▶ Make the style conversational and inclusive and, most importantly, exciting while still remaining essentially informative.
▶ Test out your feature on a child volunteer and get feedback – be prepared, children are often shockingly honest.

14

....

Writing for television and radio

In this chapter you will learn:
- *the differences between print and broadcast styles*
- *how to write for radio*
- *how to write a documentary for television*
- *the benefits of podcasts.*

If you want to write non-fiction for the broadcast media, you will have to cultivate a different set of skills than those needed for print journalism. Although there is some overlap in writing style, writing for the spoken word and to length/time-constraints requires some additional disciplines. In the past, writers for both radio and television were taken on and, even if they had completed journalism programmes, most of their training was done on the job. In the current economic climate however, staffing levels are at the bare minimum and most editors are not able to afford the time to train new people to the profession.

The good news is that there are other ways to cut your teeth in the field of broadcast journalism. The most important skill to get under your belt is the ability to communicate effectively, clearly and concisely. If you can master this skill and get some airtime in return, then there is a range of possibilities for freelance writing for radio or television.

Writing for radio

There are three different categories of writing for the radio:

▶ writing commentary (opinion or insight features)

- ▶ creating scripts
- ▶ reporting news items.

Realistically, it is extremely difficult to break into radio script writing, especially if you have no broadcast writing experience. Given that this book is aimed at novice writers, we will concentrate our efforts on writing commentary and news items, which stand a better chance of acceptance. As in print journalism, radio stations use freelance radio reporters. Naturally, you would be expected to have your own quality recording equipment if you plan to work as a freelance radio reporter.

One of the biggest differences between writing for radio compared to writing for say a newspaper or magazine is the story length and, as a consequence, the detail that you include. If you are writing for the print media, a feature can run to several thousand words. As a writer for the radio, you will be lucky if a news story exceeds 100 words and a commentary runs to 700 words.

Insight – writing to time

Whether you are writing a news item or a full script for the radio, you will have to start to think in time allocation rather than word counts. Don't worry, as this will become second nature to you as time goes by and your experience grows.

CONDENSING YOUR MATERIAL

For commentary and news, you must be extremely concise in your writing style – you need to identify the key elements of the story and abandon all other details. For those who are thinking that only having to write a couple of hundred words must be easier, you should think again. Any journalist will tell you that it can be harder to write to a tight word count.

Let's imagine that you want to write a script for a story about a forthcoming community event to submit to your local radio station rather than simply sending them a press release (see later in this chapter). If you were submitting a news story to a local newspaper, 125 words would be considered brief. However, even that is far too long for radio.

A radio news story generally runs for around 20–30 seconds. As a rough guideline, you can work on a rate of approximately 155 words per minute (wpm) for the typical spoken word. (A rapid-fire radio advertisement is read at around 180 wpm and 200 wpm is the maximum possible.) When counting up the length of your script, numerals and symbols and so on each count as one word; a 30-second story about your community event is only going to be 77 words long. Given how few words you have to play with, it is essential that you get to the heart of your story straight away and leave any superfluous details out.

WRITING STYLE

If you are writing for radio broadcast, you should use language that sounds like everyday speech and choose a sentence structure and vocabulary that is appropriate for your listenership. In essence, keep your language simple and conversational, without becoming too informal.

Stay present

It also helps to write in the present tense, as this gives an energy and immediacy to your writing, and helps the listener to feel that the story is of-the-moment. Even if you are describing an event that has already taken place, if you use the present progressive tense (for example, 'Strictly Come Dancing contestant John Sergeant is calling it quits') you still manage to keep that feeling of immediacy.

Keep sentences simple

Avoid compound or complex sentences and, wherever possible, stick to simple sentences. If you have forgotten basic school grammar, a simple sentence means a sentence containing a subject and a verb. That is not to say you can never use a compound sentence (two simple sentences joined by a co-ordinating conjunction such as 'and', 'but' or 'nor') or a complex sentence (two simple sentence joined by a subordinating conjunction such as 'when', 'because' or 'although') but your report will be much clearer if you keep these complex and compound sentences to a minimum and concentrate on using simple sentences.

Avoid the passive voice

Simple sentences that use active verbs are far more effective for radio than passive sentences. By the same token, if you introduce a sentence using a 'there is' or 'there are' construction, you are wasting words and time. Make sure the 'subject' is doing something, so keeping the sentence active. For example, 'There is a £25,000 grant being offered to The Roundall Theatre Company, which should prevent them from closing down' becomes 'A £25,000 grant awarded to The Roundall Theatre Company will prevent closure.'

Avoid relative clauses

Lastly, at the risk of sounding like a grammar teacher, you should avoid using relative clauses in the middle of your sentences. These are clauses that interrupt the sentence using words like 'who', 'which' or 'where' and provide additional information about the noun in the sentence. For example, 'Arnold Schwarzenegger, who had a successful Hollywood career taking leading roles in films such as *The Terminator* and *Predator*, later became the Governor of California.' This is fine in print journalism because the reader can cast their eye back to the beginning of the sentence if they lose the thread. A listener cannot do the same, so it is up to the writer to keep sentences concise and uninterrupted. Thus, for radio, the above sentence might read 'Arnold Schwarzenegger had a successful Hollywood career taking leading roles in films such as *The Terminator* and *Predator*. He later became the Governor of California.'

Keep it easy to interpret

Even if you send an MP3 clip of your story together with your script, there is a chance that the producer may want an in-house talent to read your item. So make sure that it is easy for anyone to interpret. This means writing exactly what you want the listener to hear. Spell out all symbols, so that '£50' becomes 'fifty pounds' and numerals are written out in full, for example, 'eighteen pounds and ninety-five pence' or 'call oh-eight-hundred-four-two-four-two'.

Rewriting news items

If you submit a news story that is read out in the morning, there is every chance that the radio station will get back to you asking for an update for midday, and if the story is still running, another update for the evening news slot. Rewriting is a common occurrence in radio journalism, so you will have to get used to adapting your stories so they reflect the current situation and you can shift the focus accordingly.

Insight – get on top of pronunciation

There is nothing worse than hearing a news item on the local radio in which the name of a local business or location is mispronounced. If you submit a story to the radio, include the phonetic pronunciation at the end of the item, so that unusual names are correctly pronounced by the reader.

REVIEW

There is only one way to check the length and sound of your copy and that is to read it out loud. You may feel silly sitting in a room on your own speaking out loud, but it is better than feeling small when an editor tells you that your copy is longer than you claim. If you overrun, then you have time to edit down your copy.

Reading out loud is also the best way to make sure the language sounds fresh and easily comprehensible, and that there are no typing or grammatical gaffes. Bizarrely, you pick these up when reading out loud but the eye can skim over them when reading silently. Once you are happy with what you have written, it is time to make a submission.

RADIO SUBMISSIONS

If you have a story that you think a radio station might be interested in, then it is customary to send an email to the relevant news editor or the producer of a particular show that you wish to target. Keep your pitch brief, simply outlining the salient points of the story and why you think it would be great for this particular station. If you send a massive tome or a script that runs to dozens of pages, then it will get dumped because editors/producers do not have time to read or listen to lots of lengthy material.

At the submission stage, there is no need to send in audio. If the station likes your pitch, it will contact you and either send you out with professional gear to get the story or ask you to send the text and possibly an audio clip, usually as an MP3 file.

If you are targeting a specific radio station, or even a particular show, then it is essential that the style of your story is in keeping with the nature and style of the programme or station. There are 40 BBC local radio stations, and over 250 commercial stations (known as ILR – Independent Local Radio stations) in the UK, so there are plenty of outlets for your submission. However, if you find that you are constantly rejected due to lack of experience (yes, I know, that hoary old chestnut again), you could try volunteering your services at a hospital or community radio station. Most cannot pay you, but they will usually cover your expenses. It is a great way to get the necessary experience of writing for radio and can be great fun as well.

Volunteering for local hospital and community radio could well result in a portfolio of work to show to commercial and local public service radio stations. You are unlikely to get rich as a freelance writer for radio but you never know where your radio experience might lead. A book publisher may hear you on the radio and become interested in your work, or you could transfer your radio skills to helping non-radio businesses to create podcasts (see below).

Insight – tune in

Just as you would never pitch to a magazine or newspaper that you are not familiar with, don't pitch to a radio show that you have never listened to. A producer will spot your lack of research immediately. So make sure you tune in before you contact the station with your ideas.

Producing a podcast

Anyone who is familiar with the websites iTunes and YouTube cannot fail to have seen a podcast. It is a mini radio show that you record and put on the internet for download onto iPods or other MP3 players. If you are not a regular on these sites, then check out iTunes.com and go to the 'podcast' section to sample a podcast for yourself.

A typical podcast, if there is such a thing since there is such enormous diversity in this field, lasts about 15 minutes to an hour, and it can be on just about any topic you can imagine, as long as you do not infringe copyright laws. You can post a podcast as frequently as you like, and the vast majority are free, although occasionally you are asked to pay a subscription.

Why am I telling you about podcasts? Well, writing a regular podcast is a great outlet for creative expression and a fun way to gain experience as a writer. Just like a blog, potentially you can reach a large number of people and, if your podcast proves popular and gets a following, you could attract the attention of a radio station or a book publisher.

Even if these leads do not come good, at least you have the satisfaction of knowing that you are gaining a name in your arena, and you can use the feedback from your listeners to inform your writing and future podcasts.

HOW TO MAKE A PODCAST

If you fancy having a go at podcasting, do not be put off by the fact that you do not have a beautifully trained recording voice or that you do not speak pucker Queen's English. This is not a handicap in podcasting. It is the content of your message and the way you present it that matters. As long as you let your personality shine through and have something to say that you care about, people will forgive imperfections in your accent and recording quality.

To get started, you simply need a microphone, a computer and some recording software that is free to download from www.audacity.sourceforge.net. If you have an Apple Mac computer rather than a PC, check out GarageBand, which comes with the reasonably priced iLife software. This is designed to help you to easily make recordings and to add jingles and intro music, which is all included in the price. It also has an editing facility.

> **Insight – video blogs**
> A visual extension of the blog or podcast is a vlog (video blog). Using a video editing program on your computer such as iMovies, you can create short films and upload them free to sites such as MySpace, YouTube and Google. Who knows where your writing and directorial skills could lead you?

Irrespective of whether you are working on a Mac or a PC, once you have written and recorded your message, you then upload your recording to a hosting site such as iTunes, and the public are now able to access it at their will. If they like what they hear, they can subscribe so that they are notified whenever you add a new episode to your podcast.

Rather than writing a vast tract of information in one go, you are better writing and recording in small segments. This approach is more likely to keep your listeners' attention. You signify a change in segment or direction by interjecting a sound effect or brief snatch of music. Why not break up the sound of your own voice by putting in interviews with other people, or inviting a friend or colleague to read a short item. If you have a lot to say in one podcast, you can break the subject into two parts, and encourage people to tune in again for the next episode.

Writing for television

Writing for television is one of the hardest fields of all to break into; it is such a cut-throat market. Many writers for television gain experience in another field first, especially radio, and then transfer across to television. Alternatively, some writers make the decision to take a job in the actual production side of television and then hone their skills and prove their worth from within the medium. However, it is by no means impossible to enter factual television via the freelance route, so do not give up hope. Writing non-fiction for film is very different to writing for print though, and there are quite a few additional aspects such as visuals and sound that you must take into account. Apart from that, the processes that you go through to produce a finished piece of writing are the same.

Television news teams do use freelance contributors (known as 'stringers') but most of these journalists have some training and experience. If you want to break into writing for television, why not consider writing a factual documentary script, where the following considerations might prove useful.

RESEARCHING YOUR FILM

Although it sounds obvious, the best place to start your research is to watch television programmes in the same genre as your proposed script. Ask yourself what works and why. What style is popular currently? What techniques do these film-makers use that appeal to you? Next it is time to get down to researching the subject of your documentary. It goes without saying that your research has to be extremely thorough and in-depth. In fact, the best quality for a documentary researcher/writer is an enquiring curiosity and a genuine desire to learn more about the subject of your documentary. In order to excite your viewers, your enthusiasm for the subject must show through. As you delve into the subject, you can ask yourself some important questions, such as:

▶ If I were in the audience, what would I want to know?
▶ Is everything I have been told the truth? How much do I need to verify?
▶ Is there something new or little known to tell on this subject?
▶ Is there anything else I need to know about this subject?

THINGS TO BEAR IN MIND BEFORE WRITING

Before you even start to write, there are many factors that contribute quite significantly to the nature of the script you will write. It is useful to give thought to these considerations before you put pen to paper, so to speak.

Subject is king Your documentary is, by its very nature, issue-specific and so your choice of subject matter is crucial to the success of your documentary film.

Be flexible Because documentaries deal with fact, not fiction, and are shot in the real world, even the best-laid plans can be upturned. Often the film-maker is unable to control the scene they are shooting or the circumstances surrounding it, so it is hard to decide how the film will turn out eventually. A flexible approach is the only option when working on non-fiction scripts.

Think visual Everything that you write will be seen and heard as images on a screen, so you must be able to write visually. Although your narration is important, the visual takes primacy. So, if something is shown visually, there is no need to mention it. For example, there is no need to tell the audience that the subject is a fireman if he is wearing a fireman's uniform and riding in a fire engine. Your narration should say what the visual does not say, and it should be in tune with what is taking place on the screen.

New worlds During your documentary, you can show details that are not available to the usual non-fiction writer and his audience. Whether it is the inside of the core of the earth or an uncharted part of a remote island, the camera can give us access. This opens up a whole new world to the viewer and, as the writer, you must make sense of it for them.

The power of documentaries Through the film medium, you are able to send powerful messages to your audience. Documentaries have long been used to inspire a change in attitudes, both socially and personally; do not underestimate the power of your documentary and give careful thought to the message you intend to convey.

Maintain credibility In order to gain and keep your audience's trust, you must always provide credible information and sources grounded in thorough and painstaking research.

Remain realistic Nice though it would be to film a re-enactment of the Battle of Thermopylae for your documentary on the Spartans, that would involve the cost of sending a film crew to Greece plus accommodation, hiring thousands of extras and, in all probability, the budget will not stretch to that. More realistically, you could show sandaled feet running through sand, a sword or shield crashing to the ground and have a soundtrack of clashing weapons and shouting/screaming, overlaid by a historian telling the account of the battle. Keeping a realistic weather eye on budget and for whom the script is intended (the target audience) is imperative.

Insight – keep abreast of new media developments

I am a luddite by nature but I recognize the fresh opportunities that new media such as podcasts, radio and television can offer to writers, so I try to keep abreast of developments by signing up for free newsletters at technical and new media-oriented websites. They are surprisingly interesting.

WRITING A GRIPPING SCRIPT

Finally, you have now reached the stage where you are ready to write. So, what makes a good script?

What's your angle? You know your subject but an inspired and creative treatment of the idea might make it stand out from the crowd.

Keep on track Don't forget the key message of your film and make sure everything you include is relevant.

Good character The main character(s) of your script – be it human, animal or even object (a hurricane) – is central to your story and it is crucial that you portray their true personality and tell their story with feeling and honesty.

Telling your story You have to decide who is going to tell your story. The narrative (aka point of view or POV) can either be told in the first person, where it is the direct point of view of one or more of your characters and the narrator speaks in terms of 'I', or in the third person. This is the more classic style of documentary where an anonymous narrator tells the story.

Go for the emotion Although you are dealing in facts and reality, there is no reason why you should not make your documentary an emotional journey for your viewer. You want them to empathize with your characters and to care about your themes, so do not feel guilty about putting them through the full gamut of emotions.

Keep it simple It is a temptation to make stories over-complicated and to over-intellectualize the narratives with long words and fancy sentences. All this achieves is to confuse or even alienate your audience; far better to stick to a straightforward, simple narration that is in tune with other elements of your film.

Have a plot Although this is non-fiction, you are still telling a story so you need a beginning, middle and end for your story.

Your audience wants to see what happens, so the story has to unfold. As in all writing, you need to hook the viewer with a strong opening, maintain the pace of your story by compelling action and make sure you finish on a high. If you can arrange for a climactic ending, where issues are resolved, even better. However, this does not mean that you have to spoon-feed your audience. Your script should allow the viewer to draw their own conclusions about events and the story you have told.

Structure Each medium comes with its own way of presenting scripts and television is no different. If your work is to be taken seriously by a production company, it will have to be laid out in the conventional format. You can find examples of scripts for television shows and their layout (albeit mainly fiction) at the BBC Writersroom (www.bbc.co.uk/writersroom) and simplyscripts.com websites.

You can also buy software for script-writing which can make your job substantially easier. Specialized software packages such as Final Draft or Microsoft's Screenplay Template (free to Microsoft Word users) are recommended. Alternatively, you will find Scriptsmart, a set of Microsft Word templates and macros for formatting scripts, at the BBC Writersroom site.

TELEVISION SUBMISSION

For writers with a proven track record, it is customary to email a production company with an outline of the idea for your film, which you can then discuss in more detail with them if they show signs of interest.

However, it is the same old story as with other forms of writing. Most production companies are unlikely to take a punt on an unknown talent, so you may be obliged to write your script and then submit it to targeted companies. Some companies will not read unsolicited scripts, namely scripts that have not been commissioned or submitted through an agent, but it is by no means across the board and some companies welcome scripts and proposals, including those from novices.

Before you send out your script, do some research into which production companies are the best match for your subject matter. After all, you are unlikely to get much interested in your drug trafficking documentary if you send it to a company that specializes in heart-warming documentaries about animal hospitals. Once you have found a good match, give them a call to try to get the name of the person in the company that you should send your script to – sometimes receptionists are tight-lipped about giving out names, but it is worth a try.

Also check whether your target production company issues guidelines on how to present a script. Most companies are happy to accept the standard presentation, as long as it is clearly typed and well presented, but it would be a shame to ruin your chances just because you failed to make a few alterations to the appearance of your script.

Protecting your work

Writers new to the business often ask me what is to stop a radio or television company from stealing your idea if you send them your script. Unfortunately, the answer is that there is not much you can do to protect your ideas, although in reality, it is a rare occurrence.

If you are concerned, there are a few precautions you can take. For example, you can send a copy of your script to yourself via registered post and leave it unopened, there are websites that will store your work and a solicitor will date stamp and store your work for a fee.

Even if you go to these lengths, it is difficult to prove that an idea is your own. If a production company broadcasts a programme that is very similar to an idea that you sent them months previously, they might argue that it was simply a coincidence and that they had been considering the idea for over a year. By all means, take a few self-protective precautions if it gives you peace of mind, but it is better to get your script out there where, if it is well crafted, it may get some interest rather than keeping it under lock and key and never getting it broadcast.

Insight – read aloud

Just as with radio scripts, if you're writing for a television documentary, it is essential that you read your script out aloud to reveal how it will sound when broadcast. Don't be shy now.

RADIO NEWS EXERCISE

▶ Produce a news piece for radio.

▶ Decide on a subject – perhaps a news story that you have seen in a local newspaper.

▶ Write a two-minute news item on the story, bearing in mind the formula for the rate of speaking is 155 wpm.

▶ Using a dictaphone or voice recorder on your phone, record your news item as you read it aloud.

▶ Check it to see how close you are to the target of two minutes (a second either way is permissible).

▶ If you are well wide of the mark, edit or rewrite accordingly and try again until you have a great news story that gives all the necessary information in the allotted two minutes.

15

Writing for business

In this chapter you will learn:
- *how to write a press release*
- *how to create promotional material*
- *ways to start a company newsletter*
- *how to enliven reports.*

When you think about a career of writing non-fiction, writing for business may not be your first choice, but it can be a valuable exercise in writing to deadlines and in a specific style, and sometimes it can lead to other things in the writing field.

Like most forms of professional writing, if you have no experience of writing for business, you will find yourself in a catch 22-situation. No company will give you work without you having some relevant experience, and you have no way to gain that experience if no one gives you a chance to prove yourself.

So this is where you have to take the initiative. In order to get some published work in your portfolio, you are going to have to be bold, possibly even pushy. Firstly, you should call in a favour from any local contacts that you may have. Do you know anyone who runs their own business, however small? A nail salon or a car spraying garage, for example? Approach them with a deal, but be honest about your motives. You need some published work. What's in it for them is that you will write some promotional material for their business free of charge. They only have to bear the production costs, which they would probably be spending in any event. Volunteer your writing services to as many known contacts as you can until you have a small collection of published work and a 'portfolio' of clients.

If you have absolutely no personal contacts to approach, you can contact small local charities and other small organizations in the public or voluntary sector. Members of staff in smaller charities and voluntary organizations are often stretched to capacity, and the offer of your promotional writing services free of charge may be very attractive. It also gives you the experience that you need.

Once you have some published work under your belt and a few company names that you can mention as being ongoing clients, you are in a position to start approaching other businesses in the area where you have no connections.

Selling your services

For many, the thought of singing your own praises to a stranger is probably a complete anathema. However, if you are unable to sell your services in this way, you are unlikely to cut it in the competitive world of business. You must be able to promote what you do, and what benefits your services will reap for a potential client, if you are to stand any chance of persuading them to employ you. If you are too self-conscious to do so, then perhaps this is not the field of writing for you.

You can approach the company owner, if it is a small business or the marketing director if it is a larger concern. Send them an email or a letter that:

▶ introduces you
▶ explains the services you can provide, for example writing press releases and promotional material
▶ outlines how your services might benefit this particular company
▶ points out that you have enclosed some samples of your published work and a client list (only if suitably long).

Be prepared to follow up this initial approach with a phone call where you can expand on the services and benefits you offer. If interested, one of the first questions a potential client will ask is the cost. You should be prepared for this. Make sure you have researched the rates of your competitors and offer a similar, if slightly preferential, introductory rate.

Registering your services with the local chamber of commerce or branch of The Forum of Private Business can be a way of getting your services known to additional clients.

Types of material

There is a broad range of written material that comes under the banner of business writing. Many smaller companies simply do not have staff dedicated to or qualified to perform this valuable function, and yet all businesses need to advertise and promote their services/ wares or welcome good publicity.

PROMOTIONAL MATERIAL

There is so much scope for a writer in this area alone, since most companies are producing catalogues and promotional leaflets throughout the year. You only have to consider how many promotional leaflets drop through your letterbox each and every day ranging from double glazing companies to local restaurants to realize there is a wealth of opportunity for the business writer right here.

Instead of putting this promotional material in the bin, get into the habit of reading the leaflets and fliers. Assess which ones work for you and why, and by the same token, which ones fail to convince and again, why? This will help you to hone your own business writing skills.

As a general rule of thumb, you will notice that good promotional material is snappy, direct, easy to understand, and it grabs and maintains your attention. You have to be able to get the message across in the headline or the first sentence. This is a tall order for any writer, but it is not impossible. Remember to engage directly with the company's potential clients, so you can address questions directly to them, as if in conversation. For example, 'Do you have a room that needs decorating? No job too small.'

PRESS RELEASES

It is generally acknowledged that readers of newspapers and magazines and radio listeners pay more attention to and are more likely to believe editorial coverage than they are an advertisement. With that in mind, it is small wonder that companies prefer to get free press coverage of forthcoming events and new developments rather than paying for an advertisement.

However, it is not enough for a restaurant to simply ring up to let the local media know that they have a new chef arriving from a restaurant in London; you would simply be redirected to the advertising department. What is needed is a press release that tells a story and that can be sent to all the relevant local or even national press. If the story is sufficiently eye-catching and novel, the journalist will follow it up and print the item in a forthcoming issue.

In days of economic boom, companies often retain the services of a public relations (PR) company to publicize their activities. However, in a more difficult economic climate, a PR company is one of the first things to go when a company tightens its fiscal belt – and smaller companies probably never had a PR consultant to start with. This is where your writing service comes into its own, because the need for publicity is still pressing, and a freelancer who can write press releases is a valuable asset.

Style

An editor's first responsibility is to his or her readers. Therefore, s/he is only interested in the story, not in giving a company free advertising. With this in mind, it is worth reassessing how you present the facts. Basically, you are writing a story, not selling something. So, always try to find the personal angle and what makes the story exceptional. If the press release is essentially about an object, development or company, then look at the people involved and see if you can tell the story from the human perspective. For example, 'Potts bookshop reports strong sales' is not much of a story; in fact, it is an advertisement. If you say, 'Potts bookshop avoids job losses as sales rise 10 per cent' it becomes more interesting; and if you were to say, 'Potts bookshop avoids job losses thanks to success of local writer Mary Baker's new book' you have got a human interest story.

Content

Like all of us, journalists are busy people and they are always looking for ways to make their job easier. A well-written press release is likely to be reproduced without the need for rewriting, which saves the journalist work. So think of each press release as a short feature in itself. If it is going to be cut at all, it is usually the final paragraphs that are dropped, so make sure you make all the important points in the first few paragraphs. The essential ingredients of a good press release are:

- ▶ a punchy, eye-catching headline
- ▶ a human interest angle (i.e. write about the people, not the product; tell the story)
- ▶ outline background information on the person, including a quote from them if possible
- ▶ do not waffle, become too technical or get bogged down in irrelevant detail; stick to the main point
- ▶ include a good photo that will catch the readers' attention
- ▶ make sure the press release is dated so the journalist knows how current it is
- ▶ include contact name and details for further information
- ▶ if applicable, put an embargo date.

Contact

You could have written the best press release in the world, but if it is sent to the wrong person and ends up on the wrong desk, it will never see the light of day. Make sure you get the name of the relevant journalist or editor and address your press release directly to them (including their job title). You can then follow it up with a polite phone enquiry to check the person has received it a few days later.

Insight – encourage follow-up

Over the years, I have received some interesting press releases that I have wanted to follow up, only to find there were no contact details. Hard to believe I know but you'd be surprised how often these basic details are omitted. Needless to say, these stories never made it into the magazine.

COMPANY NEWSLETTER

A company newsletter is a great way for senior management to keep staff and clients up to date with what is happening within the organization and to fanfare staff and company achievements. They come in a wide variety of shapes and sizes, ranging from a simple A4 page to elaborate, glossy magazines.

Although professional freelance writers are sometimes used, most company newsletters are written and produced in-house, often falling to the human resources or marketing department. If you work for a large company that produces a newsletter, why not volunteer to be involved? It is good writing experience.

A newsletter is also comprehensive so keep an open mind about what you might be asked to do: you may get to interview personnel or clients, or you could find yourself covering events and functions at various locations and times, including evenings and weekends. Being involved in a company newsletter can become time consuming. One of the most complex parts of compiling a company newsletter is getting all contributions in on time, collating the material and editing it to fit the space available. This is effectively an editing job, albeit on a small scale, and it is useful experience if you eventually want to go into print journalism.

COMPANY OR MANAGEMENT REPORTS

Traditionally, management reports are written in overblown, long-winded prose and they are usually written in-house by middle managers who adore this dated, self-important style of writing. However, increasing numbers of companies are waking up to the fact that these reports simply alienate their shareholders and members of staff, and a few are now employing the services of a freelance writer to inject a more accessible tone, using plain English, into what can be a stultifyingly dull report.

It is perhaps a long shot, but should you get a chance to write a company or management report, try to write it in concise, everyday English that everyone can understand. However, be aware that although a company might think it wants change, it probably does not want anything too radically different – and they are paying your bill – so walk the fine line between a new approach and a style that will not ruffle too many feathers.

COMPANY HISTORY

If a company is approaching a major anniversary, it may decide to commission a company history. In fact, if you know a local firm has a big anniversary coming up, why not be proactive, and contact them to suggest a company history might be a good way to celebrate.

You will get a brief from the client but, in general, a company history shows the evolution of the company from inception to current day, and carries interviews with key personnel and customers. It can be an interesting project, but time consuming, as you will have to conduct interviews and write them up, go through company archives and track down suitable clients/former employees for quotes. Make sure you factor this additional research time in when you agree a fee for the project.

PRESS RELEASE WRITING EXERCISE

▶ Write a press release for a forthcoming event that is taking place at your work, or the children's Brownie group, or whatever takes your fancy.

▶ Once you have completed the release, including your contact details at the end and all the relevant dates and information, show it to the event organizers for feedback.

▶ Whether you intend to send it or not, go through the motions of finding the name, title and contact details for the appropriate editor/journalist at your local newspaper or radio station.

▶ If you decide to send the press release, make sure you have the organizer's permission.

16

Collections, anthologies and graphic novels

In this chapter you will learn:

- *how to write and compile an anthology*
- *how to find contributors to your anthology*
- *how to write a non-fiction graphic novel*
- *what part the visuals play.*

When you think of anthologies and graphic novels, your mind probably turns straight away to collections of fictional short stories and comic book tales. However, non-fiction does surprisingly well in the collections genre, as witnessed by the high sales of anthologies of personal experience stories. There are also increasing numbers of publishers that are turning to graphic novels as a way to depict difficult and contentious issues in a different, and some would say less confrontational way.

Both approaches offer opportunities for new writers because the field is not as saturated with proven talent as some other genres of writing. If you are artistic, you could even consider writing and illustrating a graphic novel on your own. More commonly, a graphic novel is a collaboration between a writer and illustrator. For those of you who like to write but also to edit and organize, compiling an anthology could be a perfect outlet for your skills. Most importantly, there are publishers who specialize in these fields who are more inclined to take on new talent, so the opportunities are there.

Anthologies and collections

An anthology is a collection of selected writings by various authors on the same subject, whereas a collection tends to be themed stories that have been researched, found and written up by one author.

The beauty of an anthology or collection is that it really can be a number of stories about absolutely anything. If you have a specialism or particular interest in a subject that you think would interest others, you could be well placed to write and compile an anthology. Or perhaps you have a cause to promote or a health issue to highlight? Whatever theme you choose, you must have a passion for the subject; it is probably the most important criterion.

Each story within an anthology stands alone with a beginning, middle and end. You will be aiming to collect together between ten and twenty stories that are roughly 1,500 to 3,000 words in length. That means that each contributor has very little room to tell their story, so it must be punchy, compelling and well written, and you must choose styles and approaches that complement each other and flow seamlessly together.

By comparison, in a collection, you can include stories of any length within a given chapter. For example, in a collection of amazing survival stories, you may choose to put snippets of news stories alongside longer accounts of derring-do and simply group the stories together under different chapter headings such as survival in the mountains, survival in the desert, survival at sea, and so on.

GETTING SUBMISSIONS

Unlike being the sole author of a collection, when you write and compile an anthology, you are involving many other people in your project, so good planning and organizational skills are essential to the success of your project.

Once you have decided upon a particular theme, it is time to start thinking about how you are going to get submissions to include. If you are writing about your own hobby or sport, then there is a good chance that you already have a network of contacts, especially if you are a club member. Put the word out about what you are doing and ask for contributions. Club members will tell others and the message will be passed down the chain until you are hopefully receiving interest from all over the country, and possibly from international links too.

If you do not have this ready-made network, then investigate whether the particular theme of your anthology could provide leads. For example, if you were planning an anthology of stories about love at first sight, you could look at contacting dating agencies, wedding planners or even contacting registrars and vicars asking them to canvas the couples they deal with on your behalf.

Another useful way to get submissions is to create a website dedicated to attracting contributors. There are free website hosts available or it could be worth paying someone to design your site. Either way, make sure you outline what your anthology is about and provide guidelines and an email address where potential authors can reach you. Things you might consider including in your guidelines comprise:

- ▶ word length
- ▶ how many stories they can submit
- ▶ what rights will be obtained
- ▶ do they need names to be changed to protect identities
- ▶ whether there is payment or not, or will they receive a copy on publication
- ▶ a deadline date for receiving submissions
- ▶ their contact and biography details.

When the site is completed, enter its details into as many search engines as possible. You can also post the guidelines on other related websites and newsletters. Why not also create a blog or tweet to publicize your website? You could also set up a fan page on one of the social networks such as Facebook, MySpace or Twitter to generate interest.

If you are still worried that you are not getting enough response, you could join online writing groups and announce your anthology on their forums, notice boards and chat rooms. You might be surprised by how much interest you generate if you start a thread about your subject.

Whatever online route you follow, make sure you always provide links to your site so potential contributors can view your guidelines.

When looking for material for a collection, the same rules apply as those for an anthology. However, you can also use the internet, newspaper archives and record offices to research stories for inclusion as well.

Insight – find a publicity officer

When looking for case histories for any book, my first port of call is the publicity officer for leading charities associated with the topic. They usually have names of people who are happy to talk to the press and authors, and who may well be prepared to see their story printed in an anthology. You will probably have to interview these individuals rather than ask them to write their own story.

CELEBRITY CONTRIBUTORS

In our celebrity driven society, an anthology of stories that includes contributions from famous people is a popular way of fund-raising for causes and charities. A percentage or all of the proceeds from sales of the anthology are then donated to the cause or charity in question. The celebrity names guarantee publicity and in turn raise awareness, and publishers are often tempted to get involved as they see this as a win–win situation.

For example, an anthology of stories that celebrate the ups and downs of living in a give-and-take world, entitled *Thanks & Giving All Year Long*, attracted many celebrity contributors including Paul Newman, Julianne Moore and Whoopi Goldberg, with all royalties from the book benefiting St Jude's Children's Research Hospital in the USA.

In the UK, a fund-raising book entitled *Brenda's Easy to Swallow Cookbook*, published by the Mouth Cancer Foundation, won a top prize as the 'best charitable initiative'. The anthology, which includes recipes donated by celebrity chefs including Nigella Lawson, Rick Stein, Anthony Worrall Thompson and Phil Vickery, aims to revolutionize the eating habits of hundreds of mouth cancer survivors. It was written and compiled by a mouth cancer sufferer, Brenda Brady, in collaboration with the charity, the Mouth Cancer Foundation. Brenda started the book while fighting the disease and, when she died in 2008, her husband and children carried out her last wish, which was to get the cookbook published.

The downside of having big names in your anthology is that they are not always easy to pin down and they are notoriously bad at meeting deadlines due to their hectic lifestyles. So build lots of time into the lead in for getting celebrity submissions in, and always give them plenty of warning. However, this is your book and you must be true to it. If you receive a submission from a celebrity that does not fit the bill or is not up to scratch, you can work with the author to rework the story or you can tactfully reject it, but do not include any contribution that you are not happy with.

COMPILING AN ANTHOLOGY

You should check your email often so that you can answer queries and confirm receipt of submissions as they come in. Read each story immediately and earmark it as a definite, a possible or a not quite right. This reading stage is time consuming, without a doubt, but absolutely essential. You are not just choosing your stories for inclusion on the strength of their writing, although this is an important factor. You want the stories of your anthology to complement each other and to fit together well.

Generally, the three strongest stories appear first in an anthology, and these would be your sample chapters to submit to a potential publisher together with your proposal. For preference, the following stories in the book will maintain this high standard of course, but if not, then naturally you send those that stand out the most.

Once you are happy with your running order and its harmony, then you can put together a 'bio' page for each author where you list their name, their bylines, and outline their other work (including links to web pages if applicable). You can also use this opportunity to inject your personal input by writing about why you chose this particular contributor.

With a collection of stories, you must seek permissions, if applicable, and credit sources for all the stories that you plan to include.

FINDING A PUBLISHER

There are publishers who specialize in, or include anthologies and collections on their list. These are the publishing houses to target if you want to go down the traditional print route. Depending on the theme of your stories, a publisher who is strong in that particular specialization is another alternative. Send your proposal plus the three strongest stories to a named editor and point out why you think your book will sit well on their list. Alternatively, if your book contains links to numerous websites, perhaps a good e-publisher might be a better option for you, and is certainly worth considering.

Your publisher should help with the national marketing of your book but you can always contact your local radio station and newspaper personally to see if they would like an interview. Most local broadcasters and papers love to interview a local author.

Insight – enduring collections

In 2006 I compiled and published a collection of mainly humorous stories about revenge entitled, *Revenge is Sweet: Settling Scores, Getting Even and Other Ingenious Stories of Retribution*. On its publication, I was inundated with requests to do radio interviews and, six years on, I am still getting the occasional radio request because humorous anthologies are perennially popular.

If your call for submissions website is still up and running, then do not forget to put an excerpt of the finished article up with links to where it can be purchased, and with thanks to all those who contributed.

The great thing about generating interest in and publicity for your anthology or collection of stories is that you can ask the public to send you more stories in a similar vein so that you can produce a second book. If you have been flooded with submissions, you can always create a companion website that allows visitors to access stories submitted for the book that could not be included due to space limitations, and invite the public to post new stories too.

Graphic novels

The purist would argue that graphic novels are a format rather than a genre, but for those of you who are unfamiliar with graphic novels, they are basically narratives in comic book style that do not form a continuous story. Published as a book – usually 64, 128 or 176 pages – they are an anthology or collection of related pieces that tell the story lexically and graphically and the story can be fiction or non-fiction. Unlike comics, they are mainly aimed at adults, not children.

At the height of their popularity in the 1950s and early 1960s, graphic novels fell out of favour for a long time but today they are enjoying something of a revival in fortunes. Many believe graphic novels are an effective tool for simplifying real-life events and recently several writers, journalists and artists have chosen to use graphic novels as a creative way to depict serious non-fiction subjects.

Difficult or painful memoirs and biographies lend themselves especially well to this genre and represent some of the best-known examples of graphic novels, including:

▶ Marjane Satrapi's *Persepolis* (2004) about a girl growing up during the Iranian revolution
▶ Craig Thompson's coming-of-age tale, *Blankets* (2003)
▶ *Maus: A Survivor's Tale* (1993) by Art Speigelman, about his father, a Polish Jew's struggle to survive the Holocaust
▶ Joe Sacco's *Safe Area Gorazde* (2000) about a cross-section of Bosnians who are trapped in the besieged town of Grazde during the wars in former Yugoslavia
▶ *Cuba: My Revolution* (2010) by Inverna Lockpez and Dean Haspiel about how the author, a Cuban dissident, was tortured and eventually escaped the island.

However, any topic can be addressed using the graphic novel approach, from the light-hearted to tragedy. In fact, there is even a graphic novel about one of the greatest tragedies in American history: *The 9/11 Report: A Graphic Adaptation* depicts the terrorist events of 11 September 2001.

Though graphic novels are not suited to all writers (and some would say not all stories), if you have a dramatic story to tell, plus the ability to picture a story in your head or to plan out a storyboard visually, then rather than writing a film or documentary script, perhaps graphic novels would be a good alternative medium for you. Certainly, if you are a good artist, this could be an interesting option but even if you are hopeless at drawing, that is not an insurmountable obstacle as many writers and artists collaborate creatively to produce graphic novels.

COMPILING A GRAPHIC NOVEL

First and foremost you need a story to tell and it helps if the subject is something that you feel strongly about, although it does not have to be as dramatic or chilling in nature as the books mentioned above. Whichever topic you choose, you still have to go through the same research processes as for any other non-fiction book, because the story you are telling is true and it must still remain accurate, even if depicted in comic-strip style.

Depending on the subject, this could mean interviewing various eyewitnesses of a certain event, or reading all the research material available on a certain topic. Once you are sure you have all the necessary information, you can start considering how you might like your graphic novel to look. When telling a non-fiction story both in words and illustrations, you cannot simply write the words and then get someone else to draw a picture to go with your words. The illustrations tell the story visually, and your limited text presents the key details.

Since you not only have prose to describe a scene or event, but can show a scene visually too, you have to think carefully about the drawing style and colour choices, in order to evoke the right emotions while depicting events as truly and realistically as possible. It is not necessarily easy to juggle all these considerations, but well-executed graphic novels can bring greater understanding to readers by effectively communicating real places, real events and real people in words and images. If you have not considered 'comic reportage' as a vehicle for your writing talents before, let's take a look at some of the advantages and disadvantages of the genre for the writer.

Advantages

▶ Due to limited space, it can help you to write tighter, more focused copy and to eliminate superfluous information.

▶ It helps you to get your ideas clear and to identify the most salient points of the story.

▶ The addition of visuals can encourage people who would never consider picking up a book on this topic to become interested.

▶ Imagery is highly emotive and it can help your reader to get a powerful sense of feeling, atmosphere and intense emotion in a way that words alone perhaps cannot.

▶ It offers great flexibility as you are able to depict scenes using artistic imagery that did not previously exist.

▶ Sequential art can be educationally effective for young people who are visual learners and the combination of visuals and words helps them to remember most important facts.

▶ It can help you to improve your collaborative skills if working with an illustrator.

▶ It gives a greater understanding of how words and images work together to tell a story.

▶ It can be an innovative, emotive and effective approach for telling biographical, autobiographical and historical non-fiction stories, which could catch the eye of publishers since they do not see many graphic novel submissions.

Disadvantages

▶ Non-fiction writing and journalism should be objective but graphic imagery can influence a reader's perceptions.

▶ Narrative and artwork are of equal importance, so avoid allowing graphics to dominate your writing.

▶ Good illustrations and text are not a substitute for accurate research and knowledge of the subject.

▶ It is very hard to get visual representation of people right; they can easily look like characterizations, and this may dilute the impact of your message.

▶ Can drawings truly capture the seriousness of certain real-life images?

▶ Readers are not accustomed to seeing non-fiction presented in this way and do not always 'get it'.

▶ Frame-by-frame graphics take up a lot of space, so are less economical to produce than prose alone.

▶ It takes a long time to produce graphic stories, so they are not ideal for any topic that is time sensitive.

Insight – collaboration works

Working with award-winning photographer Simon Walker on my first photographic book *Para: Inside the Parachute Regiment* (Bloomsbury) was a great lesson in how to collaborate. We had to agree on how to make each element – the words and the images – work together to optimum effect.

PITCHING A GRAPHIC NOVEL

Use an annual guide such as *The Writers' Handbook* or the internet to find publishers who specialize in graphic novels, preferably non-fiction, although this may be a tall order. You can also target the publishers of comic books. Once you have identified your target publisher, get the name of the relevant editor before sending your submission. It is best to send some sample artwork and to condense your story into a plot form. You can expand on why you think a graphic novel is the best medium to convey your story and cite other successful non-fiction graphic novels.

Although growing in popularity, non-fiction graphic novels are still relatively rare, so be prepared for some resistance. However, if you have a strong idea and powerful visuals, graphic non-fiction could appeal to a publisher looking for that innovative twist to a subject.

Insight – curious classification

When looking for examples of non-fiction graphic novels in the library, I found them variously listed as 'graphics' and 'sequential art stories'. If you can't find any examples under graphic novels in the non-fiction section, it could be worth checking out these categories or get the librarian on the case.

STORYBOARD EXERCISE

Not everyone can think visually. To find out if you are suited to writing a graphic novel, try the following exercise.

▶ Read a national newspaper and select a story that captures your imagination.

▶ Write down the salient points of the news story.

▶ Now visualize how you might depict the story with visuals and text.

▶ Write a brief description of what you might see in each sequential drawing and write the text to accompany each illustration. If you are artistic, you can sketch pictures showing staging of figures and backgrounds, and write the text underneath.

▶ How hard did you find it to make a storyboard in this way? If it came naturally and you enjoyed it, then perhaps the graphic novel genre is one worth considering.

17

Routes to publication

In this chapter you will learn:
- *how to find a publisher*
- *how to find an agent*
- *how to write and submit a proposal*
- *how to check a contract*.

Everyone has heard horror stories about multiple rejections from publishers but the truth is that editors are always looking for new talent and good writing; you simply have to give yourself the best chance of getting your manuscript read and accepted. In order to do that, there are some simple rules to follow.

Finding a publisher

You have two options when trying to find a traditional publisher to produce your book. You can either find an author's agent to represent you (see later in this chapter) or you can submit a proposal and sample material yourself directly to a publisher. There are advantages and disadvantages to both choices, but let's look first at going it alone.

FINDING THE RIGHT PUBLISHER FOR YOU

Sending out your manuscript to publishers at random is a sure-fire recipe for rejection. Publishers see hundreds of unsolicited manuscripts every day. If your book does not fit their profile, it will be rejected, possibly without even being read.

The key is to find a publisher who specializes in certain markets that dovetail with your subject area. To find such publishers, go to a bookshop or search an online bookshop for books already published in your field and check out the publisher's details. If there are no direct comparisons, look for books that might appeal to a similar audience. For example, if your book is on kinesiology, then a publisher who produces books in the mind, body and spirit genre is a good bet.

You can also find contact details for publishers, plus a brief round-up of their areas of publishing expertise, in guides such as the *Writers' and Artists' Yearbook* or *The Writers' Handbook* but make sure your copy is fairly current, as it is published every year and people move around within the industry.

It is helpful to think about where your book might fit on the shelves of a bookstore, as the sales team of any potential publisher will want to be able to categorize it in this way. Naturally, some books can sit in several places – kinesiology could perhaps also be found in the alternative health section – but choose which category best fits your book and then look for a publisher with this specialization.

Once you have a shortlist of publishers who concentrate on the right area, you can prioritize which is the best option for you. You are aiming for a publisher who has books in this general subject area, perhaps from a different angle, but not a book that is too close to your own.

Another consideration is the size of the publishing house. There are advantages to being with a smaller specialist company, just as there are benefits to being with a large publisher and it largely comes down to personal preferences, although let's look at the pros and cons for each that you might like to consider.

Small publishers
▶ Your book may get more attention if the company is producing only a few titles each year.
▶ Smaller teams can often make decisions more quickly and have more flexibility so can react more rapidly and make changes more readily.
▶ As a specialist publisher, they know their market inside out.
▶ You are less likely to get a large advance from a small publisher.
▶ Smaller companies may have fewer resources for sales, marketing and distribution services.

Large publishers
- ▶ Large publishers have greater clout with booksellers, so can push for promotions and for stores to take higher numbers of copies.
- ▶ Advances tend to be higher from bigger companies.
- ▶ A recognized name can bring prestige to your book.
- ▶ Decisions take longer to be made and are harder to reverse or change in order to react to an unexpected opportunity.
- ▶ If you are a small fish in a big pond, your book may not get the promotion or attention it deserves.

Insight – specialist is best

I have had good experiences of being published by both large and small publishers but my preference is for a publisher who concentrates on a few core areas that are related such as non-fiction health, parenting and personal development, for example.

You now have a shortlist of potential publishers that you have identified as a good match for your book, but should you consider getting an agent before you make an approach?

Finding an agent

Although having a good agent can be hugely beneficial, finding and appointing an agent is not the right option for everyone. Here are some thoughts to help you decide whether or not you need an agent.

Pros

- ▶ Some publishers only accept manuscripts that come via an agent.
- ▶ Some publishers see an agent as a built-in layer of quality control, since the agent has already rejected manuscripts that stand little chance of finding a publisher.
- ▶ Agents know the publishing industry and should not only have good relationships with editors but also know what trends are happening and what publishers are looking for.
- ▶ An agent will do all the negotiating and wrangling on your behalf, leaving your author/editor relationship unsullied.
- ▶ Agents sometimes play publishers off against each other, so securing you better financial terms.
- ▶ Publishing contracts are complex and intricate and a minefield for the uninitiated. An agent can easily navigate publishing

contracts, picking up on questionable clauses and bargaining on various aspects of the deal on your behalf.

▶ A good agent should be able to advise you about your proposal.
▶ Occasionally an agent can bring new writing work your way if they hear that a publisher has a book idea and is looking for a suitable author.

Cons

▶ Finding a good agent who suits you can be difficult. The best agents are nearly always at or near client capacity, although they are unlikely to turn down a manuscript that was clearly a work of genius or an author who is marketing gold.
▶ Some agents do not add value and simply do the job that you could do yourself, while taking 10–15 per cent of your earnings.
▶ If an agent has a bad relationship with a specific editor – it happens – then it might discourage them from looking at your manuscript.
▶ Some editors, particularly in small specialist non-fiction publishing, prefer to have a direct relationship with the author.
▶ An agent is usually looking for the best financial deal for you and could steer you towards the publisher who is paying the most rather than the publisher who best suits you, your book and your future publishing opportunities.
▶ If you only want to write one book and no more, an agent may be reluctant to take you on since s/he is investing time and effort in you with no possibility of future returns.

SECURING AN AGENT

If you know that your favoured publisher will not accept unsolicited proposals or if you have weighed up the pros and cons and decided to go ahead with finding an agent, where do you start? Although there are plenty of agents, finding a good one who suits you is not easy.

The best way is through personal recommendation, although this is not available to everyone of course. Even if you do not move among the literati, you may know somebody who has contacts in publishing or who has a relative who has had a book published. Put out the word, and if you find someone who is willing to give you their personal feedback, ask them what they liked or disliked about their agent, what sort of experience they had, and whether their submissions were successful? If the experience is positive, ask their permission to mention their name when you approach their contact.

Alternatively, you could attend a writing conference in order to meet agents in person, or at least to see them in action if they are participating in a talk or a panel discussion. This would give you a feel for their modus operandi and whether or not they are a good fit for you. For those of you who do not have access to a personal recommendation, you can look for a suitable agent via the Association of Authors' Agents (AAA) whose members have at least three years' experience and use a standard agreement letter with their authors.

There are also lists of agents to be found in the *Writers' and Artists' Yearbook* and *The Writers' Handbook* and on various websites for writers. There are brief descriptions of the subject areas that each agent works in, so only consider those in your particular sphere of writing. Apart from that rather obvious caveat, other considerations such as size, their client list, how long they take to respond and whether or not they have a website, are all down to personal taste and instinct.

SIGNING AN AGENT'S CONTRACT

The vast majority of agents now charge 15 per cent of your advance and of all subsequent earnings from direct sales – domestic and foreign – of your book, although some still charge only 10 per cent. You should avoid any agent who wants to charge you to read a manuscript or for editorial services – most reputable agents offer this service for free although, not unreasonably, they would expect a preliminary letter with synopsis and stamped SAE to accompany your manuscript.

When you come to that wonderful moment when you agree that you are right for each other, the agent may want you to sign a contract. Rarely, a contract is only for the current book or project. More commonly, the contract is open-ended with a set notice period on either side (usually three months), although occasionally you may be asked to sign a time-limited contract; for example, a two-year contract which covers all work on your behalf during that period. Make sure you read the contract carefully and if there are any conditions or stipulations that you do not understand or that do not seem fair to you, ask about them or request that they are taken out of the contract before signature.

Naturally, during the tenure of the contract, you are not allowed to have your work represented by anyone else. It is generally understood that any agent who has sold a book to a publisher on your behalf will continue to represent you for that book and take their percentage for so doing, even if you have moved on to another agent.

> **Insight – keep it professional**
>
> Remember that your agent represents you to publishers. It is a professional relationship. They are not obliged to edit your work, cure your procrastination or be your confidant. Chelsey Fox of Fox & Howard Literary Agency has been my agent for over 20 years and I am happy to say that a deep friendship has developed over the years. Initially though, expect to keep the agent/author relationship on a purely professional basis.

Writing a compelling proposal

Whether you are going to submit directly to a publisher or via an agent, to stand any chance of acceptance, you must write a polished and persuasive proposal and that requires an investment of time and concentration. The aim of your proposal is first and foremost to sell your book idea but it is also to persuade the agent/publisher that you are the right person to write the book and that you have the necessary credentials (namely knowledge and experience) to do so.

As s/he reads your proposal, the publisher wants to be able to satisfy him or herself that:

▶ there is a market for your book
▶ your book has something to offer readers
▶ you are qualified to write it
▶ it is well-placed within the competition
▶ it catches the zeitgeist and is not too early or late.

It is your job to make sure you answer all these questions in your proposal and its covering letter.

ELEMENTS OF A GOOD PROPOSAL

Over the years, I have written numerous proposals, many of which have been accepted while some have not. I have found that including the following information, under these or your own headings, will cover all the details that a publisher or agent might expect to see. Keep your writing clear, concise and accurate – after all, they will be judging you not just on what you say but how you say it.

Title page This contains the title of your book, your name and your contact details. You may not have given much consideration to a title, or simply had a working title in your head, but now is the time to give a title some careful thought. It would be too much to suggest that a bad title is a deal breaker, but if you come up with something catchy that sums up your book, a publisher will be impressed.

Sometimes it helps to have a snappy title and a strapline which explains in more detail what the book can do for the reader. For example, my book on dealing with ageing parents was entitled *You and Your Ageing Parent: How to Balance Your Needs and Theirs*. If you really cannot come up with anything, then put a straightforward descriptive title and put 'working title' in brackets after – at least this shows that you are aware it is not a stunning title and that you are open to suggestions.

Introduction This should be four or five paragraphs long and is your chance to market your book idea to the publisher. This is where you include information on why the book is needed (some salient statistics can help), what it covers, and why people will buy it.

Target audience Outline who is likely to buy the book and why it will appeal to them. If you think your book has international appeal, then say so here. And highlight if your target audience has any distinguishing features that may interest a publisher from a sales/marketing perspective; for example, although the audience for a book on vintage Maserati cars may be small, they are known to pay handsomely for books offering this rare specialist information.

Competition You are required to point out what books of a similar ilk are already on the market already. However, this does not have to be a negative. You only have to mention the most recent titles and then you can point out (subtly) that continued good sales figures for these books proves there is a strong market for this subject, and that your book will appeal to this existing audience because it is written from a different angle, whatever that may be.

Marketing You do not have to have amazing connections or a celebrity name, but it does help to show that you have thought about ways to reach the market or to get publicity for your book. Hence, if you have a blog, newsletter or podcast that has a following, or if you regularly give talks on your specialist subject, then you have what is known in the trade as a 'platform'. Namely, you are able to reach a wide audience to promote your book to people who are already fans. In a similar vein, if you have any media connections or contacts with the local press, you can mention them at this point. Do not be downhearted if you draw a blank in this regard. It is not a deal-breaker – simply leave this section out of your proposal.

About the author This is where you can sell yourself to the publisher. It is not a CV, so don't include any information that is not relevant to how you are qualified or suitable to write the book. Include relevant background and credentials, brief outline of research you might have done or experience that has bearing on the book, and any previous publications. If you are an academic, resist the temptation to list your qualifications and papers unless they are directly relevant to the book proposal.

Chapter breakdown List the chapter titles followed by a brief explanation of what will be covered in the chapter. You are looking at one paragraph, or possibly two at most per chapter. It is supposed to offer just enough information for the publisher or agent to see how the book will shape up.

Sample material Together with your proposal, you should send some sample material. You only need to include a couple of chapters from your book, and it does not have to be the first two. I recommend that you send two strong chapters that are representative of the breadth of material included.

Query letter Your covering letter or query email is extremely important because it is this that will dictate whether or not a publisher or agent actually makes the effort to read your proposal. Your letter has to be tightly focused on the job in hand, which is getting the publisher or agent to read your proposal, so any extraneous information such as your academic achievements, the epiphany that led to your writing or your hobbies should be omitted. Rather, you should send a one-page letter to a named editor. The letter should comprise:

▶ First paragraph: a statement that catches the reader's attention. It could be a startling statistic, an innovative approach to a subject or a new revelation. This has a bearing on and is a prelude to a brief outline of the book's aim and content. This paragraph should pique curiosity or excite.

▶ Second paragraph: This middle paragraph – and you may need a third – is dedicated to your writing experience and/or your credentials. Essentially, explain why are you the right person to write the book – be confident about yourself but not arrogant. Include any book sale successes you may have had.

▶ Concluding paragraph: Keep this short and to the point. Something along the lines of, 'I hope you enjoy my manuscript and that it is of interest to you. I enclose a stamped, self-addressed envelope, and look forward to hearing from you.' If you are confident of success or do not need sample pages returned, forget the bit about the SAE.

I have given general submission advice here but always read the submission guidelines for a specific publisher or agent (if they have them) and make sure you follow them closely.

FINAL CHECKLIST

Before you send off your proposal, get a trusted friend to read it through and give candid feedback. Get them to proofread it thoroughly and then go through it again yourself with a fine-toothed comb looking for any spelling or grammatical errors, which will jar horribly with a prospective publisher. Then tick off the following checklist before popping your proposal into the postbox:

▶ sample chapters and proposal are typed, double spaced, page numbered, and clearly printed on white paper using standard font in 12 point size (such as Times New Roman, Calibri or Courier)
▶ your name and contact details (including telephone number) appear clearly on covering letter and title page of proposal
▶ pages of proposal are secured together either by elastic band or large clip
▶ your covering letter is single spaced, and no more than a page long
▶ stamped, self-addressed envelope (big enough to contain your package and with enough postage attached) is enclosed (if applicable).

Finally, it may sound obvious, but do make sure you put the correct postage on the package. If your proposal lands on the publisher's desk together with a demand for excess postage, it will not go down well.

Successful submissions

You are now ready to send out your proposal to publishers and/ or agents. The dilemma for new writers is whether or not to send out multiple submissions or to pick one and wait for a reply before sending to others. It is hard to say categorically one way or the other. From a publisher's perspective, most like to think that they are being approached individually. From the writer's point of view, that can entail long waits and a delay in getting published because publishers are notoriously slow in replying. So here's the rub.

My suggestion is that you send your proposal to your first choice publisher/agent. In your covering letter you can say that you hope to hear from them soon and that you will not contact anyone else for now. In a month or so, if you have not heard, you can send an email or a follow-up letter explaining that you will wait another couple of weeks but will then be trying elsewhere, but keep the tone friendly and non-accusing. That usually elicits a response, even if it is rejection. If you pester or take a high-handed approach with an editor who is probably swamped with manuscripts, you risk being labelled a pest and, if a decision is borderline, the prospect of a high maintenance author might tip the balance against you.

If you decide that you will take your chances at offending and send to all your top publishers at once, then make it clear in your letter that your manuscript is with several publishers. If it is a strong proposal, it is unlikely that this alone will prevent a publisher from taking you on.

> ### Insight – keep a copy
>
> Never send original documents to a publisher or agent without first taking copies. In fact, make sure you have back-up files on your computer as well as back-up disks that are kept in different places in your home, including a fireproof box, and even in a different location.

NEGOTIATING CONTRACTS

If you have gone down the un-agented route and you get an acceptance from a publisher, you will have to negotiate a contract. Standard book contracts tend to be 20 or more pages of inaccessible legal jargon and publishers are willing to barter over obscure points such as percentages paid on foreign book club rights or serialization rights. Book contracts are a legal minefield and far too complex to enter into in detail here. I suggest that you become a member of the Society of Authors that offers a contract vetting service or appoint a lawyer specializing in publishing to check the fine details of the contract.

You can however take a view on the more obvious and important parts of the contract, namely the deadline, advance and royalties. If you are happy you can deliver by the deadline, the next pressing issue is how much will you get paid? The publisher will make you an offer. For example, as a first-time author, they may offer an advance of £2,000: a third payable on signature, a third on delivery and acceptance of the manuscript, and a final third payable on publication. The royalties could be 7.5 per cent of net receipts. How do you know whether or not this is a good deal? Frankly, it is hard to say. In my experience, publishers are rarely trying to rip you off but there is not a huge amount of money available upfront and they are acutely aware that they are taking all the risks. Actually, there is usually some room for manoeuvring and you may be able to negotiate a slightly better deal but the figures are not going to move substantially. The only situation where that might not hold true is if you have several publishers interested in your book and they get into a bidding war. However, do not get your hopes up, as this is a rare situation for a first-time author of a non-fiction book.

Before you enter into hard negotiations, you must ask yourself whether you are keen to work with this publisher, and whether you are prepared to jeopardize the deal by holding out for a raised offer. Only you can know the answer to these questions. What I would say is that you may ask for a bigger advance or a better rate on royalties but there are also other considerations apart from the money. If this publisher is going to promote and market your book widely and has a good reputation within your chosen field, this is not to be underestimated.

SUBMISSIONS LETTER EXERCISES

Exercise one

Before writing a proposal for your own book, try writing a sales pitch for one of your favourite non-fiction books. Read the back cover blurb for inspiration and then set down three paragraphs about the book that its author might have included in his or her proposal.

Exercise two

Write a draft submission letter to accompany the proposal for your book idea. Remember to cover all the points outlined above:

▶ draw the reader in with a catchy hook
▶ explain why the book is required at this time and what makes your angle different/unique
▶ outline your strengths, experience and credentials as author and any relevant previous publishing experience
▶ Conclude the letter politely, succinctly and optimistically.

Get a friend to read your letter out loud and gauge his or her response to it, as well as listening to how it sounds and whether or not you have covered all the necessary points effectively.

18

....

What happens next?

In this chapter you will learn:
- *how to take positives from rejection letters*
- *how to stay inspired*
- *how to beat writers' solitude*
- *how writing professionally can pan out*.

You have done all you can. You have thoroughly researched your book, written a tightly crafted manuscript and a compelling proposal, both of which you have sent to a well-matched publisher. What could possibly go wrong?

Sadly, even if you have ticked all the right boxes and have a saleable book, there is no guarantee that you will get a publishing deal, at least not on the first submission. There are so many reasons why a publisher may not take on your book. Perhaps it does not sit comfortably with the other current titles on their list or they already have a book on that subject that is doing well for them. Maybe the editor is not convinced that there is a market for the book or that the genre is as popular as you suggest.

It is helpful if the editor or agent gives a reason in their rejection letter because you can sometimes glean something useful from it, but often you just simply receive a standard rejection slip with a terse 'No thank you' and no explanation. Either way, just because one editor, reader or agent does not want your book, it does not mean that another will feel the same way. These decisions are purely subjective or based on criteria within the company that are beyond your control. Although it feels devastating when a rejection letter arrives, it does not mean your book is a failure. Bear in mind the story of the best-selling living author, J K Rowling. It is claimed she received 12 rejections before her book was finally signed. Rowling will not confirm the exact number, preferring to leave the final number of rejections at 'a lot'. The Harry Potter books may be fiction but the principle of continuing to believe in your project and resubmitting is the same.

Dealing with rejection letters

It is important that you do not take a rejection from a publisher or agent personally. As a writer, you must develop mental tenacity and self-belief. Nonetheless, you can learn from rejection letters, especially if the editor gives detailed feedback. When there is something constructive in the rejection that resonates with you, you can sometimes make changes to your book for the better because of it. If the rejection is simply because the editor did not like your book, then there is nothing you need to do except to try to find someone who will. Perhaps the publisher suggests the market for your book is not big enough for a large publishing house. In that case, why not try a smaller, more specialist publisher.

If the feedback is subjective, it is up to you whether or not you take it as useful advice or whether you seek a second (or more) opinion. If you are repeatedly told that your book is too long and needs editing down, then it is probably worth losing several thousand words. If an editor tells you that you cannot write, it may be that your style simply does not appeal to them, and others would not agree.

So, when do you give up? If you honestly believe your book is publishable – and you must be completely candid with yourself here – then some would say that you have to exhaust all possible avenues before quitting. Or possibly, a different approach is required. If you have been using an agent to submit to major publishers, perhaps you could submit directly to smaller, specialist publishers instead, or vice versa. Persistence is vital but ultimately only you can know when you have had enough. While you are still in the process of submitting your manuscript to publishers and agents, it is crucial that you stay positive and confident, and wherever possible, still engaged in the writing milieu.

> **Insight – don't fight a losing battle**
> If you're thinking of arguing with a rejection letter, I wouldn't recommend it. An editor is unlikely to change their mind. The only exception to this rule is if you have some concrete new development that might make them reconsider. For example, if a celebrity or leading expert has just agreed to write a foreword or to write an endorsement for the cover.

Staying inspired

If you have enjoyed the writing process, it can leave a big hole in your life when your book is finally finished. While you wait to hear back from a publisher or agent, it is a good idea to stay inspired by keeping your hand in with some personal writing, or even to start on your next book/magazine/script project. Perversely, this is especially true after you have received rejection letters; rather like getting back on a horse after a fall. Even if you intend to persevere with submissions for the current book, writing something new or researching one of your other ideas is one of the best tonics for combating disappointment.

WRITING CLASSES

Whether you enjoy writing short news stories, travel writing, a family history or some personal writing, you will receive masses of support and inspiration along the way when you join the wider writing community. A writing class or group can help you to develop your writing skills and to feel less isolated (see Coping with solitude later in this chapter). You can also learn from the successes and failures of other members of the group, and it is remarkably uplifting to share your own writing highs and lows with fellow writers.

You can find details of local authority-run evening classes online or at the local library. Courses specifically for non-fiction writing are quite rare, but even joining a creative writing course can be beneficial as many of the techniques and skills required for descriptive writing can be used in the non-fiction genre too. The telephone call to the arts and culture department of your local council is another way to track down local classes.

You can also find inexpensive writing classes ranging from script writing to community writing workshops run by the Workers Educational Association (WEA) as part of their programme. Their website lists courses in the vicinity of your postcode and they are usually inexpensive.

WRITING CIRCLES

Joining a writing circle can be a good way to get feedback on your work from fellow writers. Naturally, you are also required to critique other people's work, but that too can be a useful exercise as it gives insight into your own writing style. These groups vary from loosely organized gatherings in members' homes to regular meetings in schools or libraries. You should be allowed to join the circle for a couple of sessions to find out if it is the right approach for you.

Whether you favour the formal or the informal style of circle, one standard given is that the feedback should be constructive and frank, but never discouraging or rude. If you find that the group dynamic is disorganized and dominated by the same voices each week, or if the comments are unduly critical, then it may be wise to seek another circle. However, in the vast majority of cases, writers' circles are supportive and productive environments in which to share your ideas and work.

RESIDENTIAL WRITING COURSES

Paying to attend a residential writing course might seem like huge self-indulgence but, in my experience as a course leader, spending time in the company of other writers, without distractions and with feedback from professional writers really can help you to make great strides in your writing. Again, there are probably more courses for creative writing on offer than for non-fiction writing but courses specializing in certain aspects of non-fiction such as life writing, journalism, creative non-fiction and script writing do exist.

One of the leading organizations in the UK is The Arvon Foundation, which has been running courses in beautiful locations since 1968. With an impressive list of tutors, their courses are well worth considering. Alternatively, you could look online for one of the overseas writing holidays, which combine honing your skills with relaxation in exotic climes.

WRITING CONFERENCES AND LITERARY FESTIVALS

Despite media parodies, these are not the domain of literary luvvies. Writing conferences and festivals provide opportunities to hear writers talking about their work and to participate in workshops and masterclasses on a broad range of topics. There will also be plenty of other writers attending, and useful writing friendships can be made during workshops, mealtimes and in the bar.

WRITERS' CONSULTANCY

There are a growing number of organizations offering professional critiques of your work for a fee. It is best to use editors who are professional writers themselves and who know the industry and specific genres of writing very well. These established and reputable consultancies will commit to read your manuscript and to provide a comprehensive, candid and constructive feedback within a specific time period.

As an editor for Writers' Workshop, I recommend that you look at the testimonials of those who have used the services of a consultancy and check the consultancy's conditions before parting with your money. You can expect to pay in the region of £250–£350 for a comprehensive critique of a full manuscript.

MENTORING

One-to-one sessions with a mentor can be hugely beneficial to the novice writer, albeit that these personal services can be expensive. Nonetheless, it is one of the most productive ways to develop your writing skills. Many of the writers' consultancies mentioned in this chapter (see Taking it further for details) offer mentoring services in addition to their manuscript critiquing provision, but there are also private organizations that offer exclusively mentoring services, such as Gold Dust. You can also look for charitable organizations who offer writers' mentoring schemes such as The Arts Council England and The Jerwood Foundation in conjunction with The Arvon Foundation but, in reality, these assisted places are relatively rare, although not impossible to find.

Insight – advice and support is invaluable

As a writing course leader and editor for a professional critiquing service, I can say hand on heart that the vast majority of novice writers who use these services get something positive from the experience. Although not impossible, it is hard going it alone and getting the advice and support of professionals plus fellow writers that you meet on courses can help to sustain you through your writing experiences.

Becoming a writer

As you have progressed through the chapters of this book, you have hopefully had an opportunity to work out what genre of writing you want to explore, decided how to write it and discovered how to submit it to the relevant person. Understanding the writing process from inception to publication should give you some insight into whether or not you want to become a professional writer, whether you have one idea that you would like to see in print in some way, or whether writing is simply a joy that you wish to keep for your personal gratification. Should you decide that you want to write non-fiction for a living, in whatever capacity, here are some tips for helping you to stay the course.

STAY FOCUSED

It can be hard to keep yourself motivated, especially when you receive more rejections than acceptances in the early days. However, keep focused on your goals, regularly review your tactics for reaching those targets, and continue to believe in yourself and what you are trying to achieve.

REMAIN TRUE TO YOURSELF

This is not simply about writing style; it is more to do with trusting your gut instinct and values. Naturally, when you are first starting out as a freelance writer, there is a temptation to say 'Yes' to everything, however unreasonable the request, because you desperately want to see your writing published. Sometimes this can mean producing a feature for no fee, just to get a byline. Yet occasionally, unscrupulous editors will take advantage of your enthusiasm and the surfeit of new writers to make unreasonable demands. If you feel that someone is exploiting your desire to be published, then do not be afraid to say 'No'. There will be other opportunities and occasionally an editor will reconsider once they realize you are not a desperate doormat. Stay true to your values, trust your instincts and you will not go far wrong.

PLAIN SAILING

You have had your first piece of work published and you have another commission in the bag. Fantastic. Will your good fortune hold? Possibly, but most freelance writers recognize that even when you are well established, you will still encounter obstacles during your writing career. Commissioning contacts move on, publications fold, it is a sad reality.

Nevertheless, if you take sensible precautions – such as not relying on a sole publication for all your revenue – and recognize that setbacks are a fact of life in the freelance world, you are better equipped to face the ups and downs of a normal writing career. It is rarely plain sailing, but the unexpected can be one of the charms of the job.

DEALING WITH SOLITUDE

We all need time and space to get in touch with our creativity and to let the writing flow but, although it can be a wonderfully absorbing and fulfilling pastime or career, writing can also be quite an isolating experience. You will spend a great deal of time alone with your thoughts and your computer. For some, the solitude can be a rare luxury. For others, it is one of the hardest aspects of the writing process.

If you find writing as a hobby quite isolating, then you must consider whether you are cut out for writing non-fiction as a career. Most freelance writers who work from home will tell you that it is a double-edged sword. Advances in communications allow an author to live anywhere; all you need is access to a telephone line and/or a postal service. Certainly, the short commute and the flexibility of being your own boss cannot be underestimated, but working on your own as a one-man-band can be a lonely career.

PEAKS AND TROUGHS

In terms of workload, it is usually feast or famine: either you are writing to tight deadlines on several features and possibly a book too, and barely keeping your head above water, or there is a dearth of commissions and you are wondering when the next job will come in.

Ideally, you need to be thinking about sending out ideas and proposals for the next commission before the current job is finished, or else the work will dry up. In reality, you are so busy meeting deadlines that there is little time to scout for new work. These time pressures are one of the major causes of the peaks and troughs of the freelance writer.

Personally, I accept that there may be some breathing space between projects and use that time profitably to do admin, to ferment ideas and to relax slightly, which may sound decadent but is essential for creative minds. If you cannot do this, try to take an hour or so every few days to concentrate on future projects and to sound out prospective commissioners.

Have fun

Writing non-fiction is one of the most satisfying ways to spend your time and it is also one of the best genres for getting published, as there are far more commercial opportunities for non-fiction writers than there are for fiction. Just look at the breadth of styles and openings that we have covered here. Whether you decide to focus on one particular genre or to experiment with others that you had not previously considered, I hope you enjoy your writing.

You may decide that you want to keep your non-fiction writing as a pleasurable but serious hobby and getting something into print would be the icing on the cake. Conversely, it may be a lifelong ambition to earn a living as a writer, and nothing less will satisfy.

Whatever you choose, remember to be enthusiastic, to take your writing seriously while enjoying the process, and to hone your skills so that you produce the best piece of writing for you, your reader and for any potential publishers.

GOAL-SETTING EXERCISE

▶ Set yourself a writing goal and a deadline to achieve it.
▶ What more can I say, you better get started.
▶ Good luck!

Taking it further

Bibliography

Eats, Shoots and Leaves by Lynn Truss (Fourth Estate)

Modern English Usage by Fowler (Oxford University Press)

Writers' and Artists' Yearbook (A & C Black Publishers)

The Writers' Handbook (Palgrave McMillan)

The Guardian Media Directory (Atlantic Books)

Willings Press Guide (Hollis Directories)

Children's Writers' and Artists' Yearbook (A & C Black Publishers)

The Self-Publishing Manual by Dan Poynter

Self-Publishing For Dummies by Jason R Rich

The Complete Guide to Self-Publishing by Tom and Marilyn Ross

Aiming At Amazon: The New Business of Self-Publishing by Aaron Shepard

Travel Writing by Don George (Lonely Planet)

Inventing the Truth: Art and Craft of Memoir by Russell Baker (Houghton Miffin)

Writing Your Family History: A Practical Guide by Deborah Cass

Writing up Your Family History: A Do-it-Yourself Guide by John Titford

Brenda's Easy to Swallow Cookbook by Brenda Brady
www.easytoswallowcookbook.wordpress.com

Publicity, Newsletters and Press Releases by A Baverstock (Oxford University Press)

Useful websites

RESEARCH

British Library
www.bl.uk
+44 (0)843 2081144

British Library Newspapers +44 (0)843 2081144

Questia (online subscription library specializing in humanities and social sciences)
www.questia.com

BIOGRAPHIES, AUTOBIOGRAPHIES AND MEMOIRS

Access to Archives Project (A2A)
www.a2a.org.uk

Family Search – a service provided by The Church of Jesus Christ of the Latter Day Saints (Mormons)
www.familysearch.org

The National Register of Archives (NRA)
www.nationalarchives.gov.uk

On this Day in History
www.historychannel.com

Oxford Dictionary of National Biography
www.oxforddnb.com

The Scottish Archive Network (SCAN)
www.scan.org.uk

1901 Census
www.1901censusonline.com

BLOGGING

www.blogger.com
www.livejournal.com
www.typepad.com
www.wordpress.com

Handbook for Bloggers and Cyber-Dissidents from
www.reporterswithoutborders.com

E-BOOKS

Adobe Acrobat
http://get.adobe.com/uk/reader/

Amazon (allows you to create a storefront that accepts orders and
processes credit card transactions)
http://webstore.amazon.com/

Directory of e-publishers
www.ebookcrossroads.com/epublishers.html

e-junkie (e-book publisher)
www.e-junkie.com

Google Checkout (processes online payments)
http://checkout.google.com/sell

Kagi (processes online payments)
www.kagi.com

PayPal (processes online payments)
www.paypal.com

SELF-PUBLISHING

www.greenbay.co.uk/advice

WRITING FOR BUSINESS

British Chambers of Commerce
www.britishchambers.org.uk

Forum of Private Businesses
www.fpb.org

RADIO AND TELEVISION

www.apple.com/ilife
www.audacity.sourceforge.net
www.iTunes.com

What happens next

Adult Residential Colleges Association (some branches run courses on non-fiction writing)
www.arca.uk.net

The Arts Council England
www.artscouncil.org.uk

Arvon Foundation
www.arvonfoundation.org

Claire Gillman
www.clairegillman.com

Gold Dust (writers mentoring service)
www.gold-dust.org.uk

Jerwood Charitable Foundation
www.jerwoodcharitablefoundation.org

The Literary Consultancy
www.literaryconsultancy.co.uk

National Council for the Training of Journalists
www.nctj.com

Open College of the Arts
www.oca-uk.com

The Workers Educational Association
www.wea.org.uk

The Writers' Workshop
www.writersworkshop.co.uk

Professional help for writers

Association of Authors' Agents (AAA)
www.agentsassoc.co.uk

Authors' Licensing and Collecting Society (ALCS) (passes on photocopying and other fees to writers of magazine articles and books)
www.alcs.co.uk

Freelance UK
www.freelanceuk.com

Journalism UK
www.journalismuk.co.uk

Media UK
www.mediauk.com

National Union of Journalists
www.nuj.org.uk

Public Lending Right (PLR) (passes on fees from libraries to authors of books)
www.plr.uk.com

Society of Authors
www.societyofauthors.net

The Writers' Guild of Great Britain
www.writersguild.org.uk

Index

Image credits